THE OTHER WAY

AN ALTERNATIVE APPROACH TO
ACTING AND DIRECTING

THE APPLAUSE ACTING SERIES

ACTING IN FILM by Michael Caine

ACTING IN RESTORATION COMEDY by Simon Callow

ACTING WITH SHAKESPEARE: The Comedies
by Janet Suzman

THE ACTOR'S EYE: Seeing & Being Seen by David Downs

THE ACTOR AND THE TEXT by Cicely Berry

ACCIDENTALLY ON PURPOSE by John Strasberg

THE CRAFTSMEN OF DIONYSUS by Jerome Rockwood

CREATING A CHARACTER by Moni Yakim

DIRECTING THE ACTION by Charles Marowitz

DUO! The Best Scenes of the 90s

FUNDAMENTAL ACTING by Paul Kuritz

THE MONOLOGUE WORKSHOP by Jack Poggi

MY BREATH IN ART by Beatrice Manley

ONE ON ONE: Best Monologues of the 90s (Men)

ONE ON ONE: Best Monologues of the 90s (Women)

ON SINGING ONSTAGE by David Craig

A PERFORMER PREPARES by David Craig

SHAKESCENES: Shakespeare for Two

SPEAK WITH DISTINCTION by Edith Skinner

STANISLAVSKI REVEALED by Sonia Moore

STYLE: Acting in High Comedy by Maria Aitken

THE VOCAL VISION: VIEWS ON VOICE

THE OTHER WAY

AN ALTERNATIVE APPROACH TO ACTING AND DIRECTING

CHARLES MAROWITZ

APPLAUSE
NEW YORK • LONDON

An Applause Original

THE OTHER WAY:
   AN ALTERNATIVE APPROACH TO ACTING AND DIRECTING
by Charles Marowitz

Copyright © 1999 by Charles Marowitz

   ISBN 1-55783-303-6 (cloth)

Printed in Canada.

Library of Congress Cataloging-In-Publication Data
The Other Way: An Alternative Approach To Acting and Directing
   by Charles Marowitz.
      p.   cm.
   "An Applause original."
   ISBN 1-55783-303-6 (cloth)
   1. Acting.   2. Theater--Production and Direction. I. Title.
PN2061.M234   1998
792'.028--dc21   97-23967
                                                            CIP
                                                             AC

British Library Catalogue in Publication Data
A catalogue record for this book is available from the British Library

APPLAUSE BOOKS

211 West 71st Street
New York, NY 10023
Phone (212) 496-7511
Fax: (212) 721-2856

FOR KOSTYA,

who I hope will never have need of it.

TABLE OF CONTENTS

INTRODUCTION

I do what works.

I believe that acting is a wilderness and that just as you reach a clearing, feeling safe and secure, it's time to march back into the wilderness.

I subscribe to no method, no school, no approach. Providing an actor can speak, move, read English, and memorize, the rest is up for grabs.

There are, of course, certain basics. You must own your lines as you own your own toes. You must know what they mean and you must mean them when you say them. But, that done, the mystery of acting will remain your lifetime companion.

I have learned most from audiences, too often ignored by actors, as if somehow doing it for them is contrary to the truth of their art. Audiences have to hear you, they have to understand you, and they must be moved to laughter or tears by what you do. It is their comfort actors must consider - their pleasure. Actors send life across the footlights and audiences send back the reward.

It is, of course, not as simple as all that. If it were, anyone could do it, and anyone can't. You need breath, stamina, skill and talent.

The first three you can acquire, the latter you can't. If you are blessed with talent, respect it and cherish it.

Young actors should, early on, rid themselves of the notion that there is a "right" way to act. There is only what works and, in order to come close to what works each night, an actor cannot burden himself with anything that does not result in the truth of the moment, and in the communication of that truth to his audience.

There is much to learn from this book and others like it, and there is much to be gained from the investigation of all theories, all styles of acting, and all approaches. But after he absorbs all he needs, the actor must be ready to forget it. He must take a deep breath, call upon his stamina and skill, trust in his talent and go out there and be.

All else is a wilderness in which the actor must happily wander.

FRANK LANGELLA

"Theatre of Cruelty", R.S.C. Experimental Group at LAMDA (London Academy of Music and Dramatic Art)   Glenda Jackson (center)

Photograph by Michael Hardy

AUTHOR'S PREFACE

Stage-direction like sex is a highly private affair and more often than not, you don't watch others doing it. Consequently, the one thing one director never knows about another is precisely how his or her effects have been achieved. I have seen staggering productions created by the most established and conventional procedures using actors who eschewed anything obscure or "experimental" in their work; who actually prided themselves on being "solid, old-fashioned actors" that learned their lines and moves and simply "got on with it." Some of the most atrocious productions I have ever seen were produced according to highly convoluted ideas based on esoteric disciplines and derived from the most unorthodox esthetic imaginable. So in positing what I call "The Other Way," I am not espousing a 'better' or even more efficacious method of work - merely one that I have personally arrived at. It seems prudent to point out that any approach that hardens into a formula has already started its drift towards obsolescence.

The motive behind much of what I do as a director is a profound dissatisfaction with the psychological and naturalistic vogue which, since the beginning of the century, has been associated with, and to a certain extent, glorified by Stanislavsky and, in America, codified by The Method. The theatre has always been cleanly divided between the 'literalists' and the 'abstractionists.' No sooner did Antoine create that den of steaming verisimilitude called Theatre Libre than Lugne Poe evoked the Theatre l'Oeuvre to challenge it. No sooner did we have Chekhov than we had Jarry. No sooner had Stanislavsky institutionalized psychological realism at the Moscow Arts than Meyerhold, Vakhtangov, and Evreinof arrived to kick it up the backside. No sooner did Brecht politicize the drama than Artaud came along to submerge it in metaphysics. The theatre, from its very inception, has always been a schizoid monster with its feet planted on the ground and its head lost in the clouds, and perhaps that has been its salvation.

The advent of naturalism in literature, then photography, then films, then television, swept theatre into a direction which esthetically confined it and stylistically confused it with electronic forms aimed at the mass audience. From the start of the century, there has been a premium on realism - whether it be Arthur Miller's brand of social realism, Tennessee Williams 'poetic realism,' Sam Shepard's 'magic realism' or David Mamet's gritty street-argot. The prominent writers have invariably been men and women shaping comprehensible and familiar modes of reality. Even poets such as T.S. Eliot, W.H. Auden and Archibald MacLeish, no matter how heightened their language may have been, have had success to the extent that they have veered towards a theatre of reasonable facsimiles. But the schizoid character of the art form has persisted - and so, in a theatrical milieu dominated by writers such as Tony Kushner, Terrence McNally and Neil Simon, one also has a wide range of Performance Artists perpetuating an esthetic whose heritage stems from Jarry, Cocteau, Picasso and other influences one would generally categorize as non-naturalistic. It would seem that no matter how deeply the theatre roots itself in the soil of realism, there is some part of it that refuses to forsake the realm of dreams, magic, myth, and poetry.

The person most caught in the middle of these divergent tendencies is the actor - who tends to be the most conservative element in the theatre. The presumption behind much of this book is that, over the past seventy-five years, the actor has not really developed his art; that his discipline is still rooted in the precepts that first appeared at the turn of this century. Whereas, metaphorically speaking, writers, poets, composers and visual artists have one foot in the 21st century, the actor is still chanting the litany of the last hundred years.

Of course, it is impossible to indict the actor without condemning his closest accomplices: the playwright, the director and the producer and so, if it is any consolation, it is a collective crime which needs to be prosecuted. But even among criminals, there are major and minor culprits, prime conspirators and 'patsies,' and by that measuring-rod, the actors are perhaps more to blame than anyone else because they have revealed a greater willingness towards complicity and less inclination to mend their ways.

The writer lives in an intellectual realm and without such habitation would never write anything worth performing. The director mediates between the writer's ideas and his own, and so he too juggles abstractions and correlates competing ideas. The actor, too often prides himself on dealing exclusively with specifics; tightening the nuts and bolts of the drama like the airline mechanic who prepares the carrier for flight but never travels anywhere himself. For generations, actors have exulted in anti-intellectualism. They have gloried in being practical, technical, detailed, down-to-earth - without realizing that an artist without concepts is like a bird without wings. The most common way of being anti-intellectual is mindlessly to reiterate precepts which have been handed down from generation to generation without recognizing that they may no longer apply - or, at the very least, require radical adaptation to new circumstances.

This book should be viewed, not like the messianic outpourings of a prophet come to lift the scales from anyone's eyes, but as the confidential musings of an intimate friend who, having seen an early rehearsal and gotten some sense of what is being attempted, proffers some advice as to what might possibly be a different way to go.

Charles Marowitz

"Theatre of Cruelty" at LAMDA (improvisation sequence)   Glenda Jackson (center)

Photograph by Michael Hardy

FROM SUB-TEXT TO UR-TEXT

Actor-training in the English-speaking world is mesmerized by the Method Two-Step - the lilt of text and sub-text. No sooner has the psychological implication of language been divined than the actor feels his artistic work has been accomplished. This is the facile legacy of one hundred years of Stanislavsky and, more than any other single factor, is responsible for the inadequacy of acting-training in America.

It is doubtful that the Stanislavsky of the early 20th century knew very much about the explorations of Sigmund Freud (despite the fact that 1898 was the year of both the establishment of the Moscow Arts Theatre and the composition of "The Interpretation of Dreams"), but we do know that the Russian was familiar with the psychological theories of Ivan Pavlov, Theodule Ribot and and possibly Jean Martin Charcot, Freud's French mentor whose terms Stanislavsky occasionally employed. More likely than not, he independently arrived at insights which were symbiotic with Freud's - which is not too difficult to do when one person is dealing with neurotics and the other with actors.

But if a hundred years of psychoanalysis and an almost equal amount of exposure to Stanislavsky-techniques have taught us anything, it is that there is a world of tumultuous experience beyond what we celebrate as psychological truth. Freud himself acknowledged this when he concocted his tri-partite division of the mind into Ego, Super-Ego and Id. According to those classifications, Stanislavsky and all his American derivatives (Strasberg, Meisner, Lewis, Adler, Hagen, etc) have taken us only to the threshold of consciousness - the realm of the *sub* or *pre-* conscious. Current Method techniques are almost entirely beyond the grasp of the id and rarely if ever descend that winding staircase to the boiler-room of human consciousness.

Theorists such as Artaud in the theatre, Jung in psychoanalysis and Campbell in mythology have dramatically charted the mysterious choreography that swirls beneath the box-steps which characterize the Method. Performances which deliver nothing more than psychological sub-text are only scratching the surface of psychic experience - certainly in the case of the Greek drama and the more finely-meshed works of the 16th and 17th centuries, i.e., the powerhouse plays of the Elizabethan and Jacobean periods. But even Chekhov and Ibsen, Strindberg, and O'Neill are inadequate when only their psychological evanescence is conveyed. The richer the play, the deeper the resonance it demands from the actor, the further it has to transcend the superficies of its language.

In training programs throughout the country, the student actor is taught how to craft an impersonation, invent character-traits, simulate plausible behavior, discover his 'actions,' devise his 'tactics' and deliver his 'beats.' Because there is no onus on him to go any deeper, to excavate the less accessible caverns that gape beneath these physical and social facades, he tends to stop his search at the very point where he should push it toward its greatest discoveries; that is, at that point where, the text analyzed and the sub-text uncovered, the mysterious abyss of the ur-text lies smoldering.

There, intellectual analysis and rational deduction forsake him. There, the swirl of the Primitive and the quagmire of the Precognitive tempt him into those inner recesses which inescapably condition both language and sub-text. There, a form of movement far removed from naturalistic behavior and a quality of sound more ancient than human speech draw him into the vortex out of which both speech and movement were originally fashioned. In any good play, all these tendrils wind their way downward into taproots that lie far beneath the social replicas that constitute the text.

Of course, the actor is not always obliged to take on such heavy-duty work. The foothills explored by writers such as Neil Simon and Alan Ayckbourn need not be approached as if they were Everest or Fuji. But if the actor is tackling the most challenging roles of the classic repertoire or some of the more elusive characters in contemporary drama, it behooves him to arm himself with something more than an ice-pick and a screwdriver. It is the very awareness that ur-text exists behind sub-text which should encourage him to go further and strike deeper, but being comfortably ensconced in a two-story house, the actor lives in blissful ignorance of castles or skyscrapers.

The great heritage of Stanislavsky (and I include here all the contemporary derivatives thereof) is to be found in playwrights such as Arthur Miller, Tennessee Williams, John Osborne, Arnold Wesker, Sam Shepard, Lanford Wilson, John Guare, David Mamet, - i.e. in the storehouse of psychological realism, and occasional departures from there that make up the *fundus* of 20th century drama. If the influence of social and psychological realism were not so pervasive, we might have a drama that did not simply try to beat the electronic media at its own game. Perhaps we would have a drama that dynamically differentiates itself from the facile verisimilitude of our *apparent* world which, when it probes the substrata of human experience, would reveal the lineaments of our inner vision rather than just the motions of our outer being.

But if this third layer of awareness exists in acting, how does the contemporary actor, practiced for the most part in conventional Method techniques, get to it? Perhaps the search is best begun within the context of some of the plays we know best.

Beneath the textual facade of 'Death of a Salesman,' there is a tangled psychic web which contains Biff's and Happy's adolescent fantasies, engendered by Willy, abetted by Linda, reinforced by a social system that glorifies popularity and abominates failure. Willy's boys are like the twisted branches of a bent tree. Their notions of success have been pre-conditioned by values inherited from America's great age of expansionism, traumatized by the blight of the Depression and falsified by the bogus optimism ushered in after the Second World War. The play's subtext is rooted in Willy's uncritical acceptance of what success in America consists of and his children are automatically measured by that same dubious yardstick.

But beneath that social and psychological terrain, there is a subsoil that vibrates with primitive rivalries which have existed for ages between fathers and sons, champions and adversaries, men and gods. Willy is not only a paterfamilias; he is also an ousted patriarch; a primogenitor dispossessed by rebellious sons. Linda is not only a long-suffering mother-hen clucking over an unruly brood; she is also a spurned queen and a dethroned matriarch.

Beneath the socio-economic structure of a family beset by the pitfalls of capitalism, there is the provider's need to sustain the welfare of his offspring and maintain the dignity of his place in the tribe. Beneath the Marxist criticism of Willy Loman's social goals, there is the fatal hubris of a man who blindly seeks to honor a deity without realizing he has been singled out as a sacrifice to its heartless creed.

In order for the depths of Miller's play to be fully plumbed, the characters need to drop through the hatchway of the sub-text into the labyrinth below. If that nether-region is achieved, it will not turn realistic drama into stylized ritual but deepen and enrich the social texture of a work whose visible surface, like all civilized artifacts, contains the markings of a deeper primitivism.

The ur-text of Miller's play is a 'given' whether the playwright consciously postulated it or not. Every social action is merely the outward show of an inner gesture which began centuries before and, just as beneath present-day Rome you may find the ruins of the ancient city on which it was built, so every social construct conceals a multitude of subterranean memories which date from time immemorial. The phenomenon of a sensibility separate from the author's but prodded into being by his work, is that magical factor which translates hieroglyphs into meaning. The mixture of actors' personalities in the batter of signs and symbols dictated by the text is what gives individuation to the performance and is why no two productions of the same play are ever alike. It is the degree to which sub-text widens into ur-text which determines the qualitative difference between one performance and another; why some productions satisfy and others are left wanting.

How does one reach this core which exists beneath the superficies of text and its facile psychological deductions? To answer that, one has to examine precisely what it is an actor does.

Using the cognitive mind, analysis, instinct and logic, the actor discerns the meanings behind a character's words and social actions. Improvisation is a tool and so is speculation. The actor formulates a theory which ostensibly explains his character's behavior and, relating it to the given circumstances, proceeds to test this theory through trial and error. When a consistent pattern begins to emerge which validates his findings, he confirms it by fixing the logic of the events that constitute his role. Sub-text *proves* text as conclusively as an arithmetical equation is proven. A consistency is established. A logic is enforced.

But we know that if there is anything certain about human nature, it is that it often flouts logic and is consistent only in being inconsistent. Indeed it is the lapse in logic, the break in consistency, the uncharacteristic action which often produces the most dramatic effect in human behavior. And when that occurs, it is the ur-text sending up a temblor, cutting a fissure into the firm-set earth.

If the actor's logical pattern is found too quickly and settles too soon, the tremors of the ur-text may never arise. To encourage their appearance, the actor must sidestep the snares of language and verifiable behavior and follow the impulses that bubble beneath. In practical terms that means using asocial sound and non-naturalistic tactics to explore the feelings that smolder beneath the sub-text.

When Hamlet confronts Fortinbras and his army en route to Poland, it peaks his sense of personal inadequacy; his lack of resolve is shamed by this young Norwegian prince's insouciant boldness. But beneath that pang of personal shortcoming other feelings lurk; for instance, the son's inability to measure up to the stature of his dead father. The moment of inferiority occasioned by the sight of Fortinbras is only the most immediate eddy of a whirlpool that winds down into Hamlet's deepest doubts concerning kingship and manhood. A courtier, a scholar, a soldier, a glass of fashion, but not an heir-apparent; not the ruler of a kingdom; not a regent as valorous, as canny, as accomplished as the father whose status, even in death, dwarfs and diminishes the paralyzed youth that bears his name. If the thrust of Hamlet's soliloquy that begins: "How all occasions do inform against me," is inspired only by a pique against the more aggressive son of another dead monarch, the moment will never express the tremulous vulnerability of a man who not only doesn't measure up to Fortinbras, but is less forthright even than Laertes and considerably less heroic than his dead father. In short, an opportunity to sound the lowest note of Hamlet's compass, what makes him most wretched and most prone to fail in his greatest endeavor, may be lost by expressing only a psychological sense of personal letdown. At the very moment the self-castigating young man is comparing himself to "this delicate and tender prince whose spirit (is) with divine ambition puffed." Hamlet feels himself an unworthy son, an abandoned child, an unprincely aberration, a disembodied spirit - the things we all feel when forced to confront our shame and uselessness, our impotence and betrayal of principle. But the actor, content with the *frisson* of sub-text, may well forfeit the richer resonances to be had from sounding the ur-text. By being content with the psychological nuance he may lose the greater, philosophical truth of which that personal pique is only a small part.

Is it possible then, to drill our way systematically beneath the sub-text?

Let's take a straightforward piece such as the Nunnery Scene from

'*Hamlet*.' First, it is a matter of gleaning the relevant action-lines which underlie the scene. For instance, we might say that Hamlet's primary action is to convey an impression of madness; the 'antic disposition' he has told us he is intending to 'put on' to help expose the plot against his murdered father. While he is playing this action, Ophelia's action may be to try reconcile the Prince that *is* with the prince that *was*, the one she previously knew and ostensibly loved. As Hamlet becomes aware that Ophelia has been 'set up' for him and that others are observing the encounter, his action may change as he proceeds to abuse Ophelia, not only to impress the onlookers but because he is genuinely irate with her for being inveigled into a conspiracy against him. As he becomes more and more abusive, Ophelia's action may change to wanting to avoid the physical violence with which the distracted prince is threatening her. As Ophelia's complicity and his mother's infidelity are mixed up in his mind, Hamlet's action may turn into a general condemnation of all women who are prone to fickleness and vacillation. When he finally discards her, Ophelia's concern may be to demonstrate her victimization at Hamlet's hands, (and thereby indicate that despite the previous liaison, she is not of the Prince's party) which takes the form of a pitiful lament against his sudden lapse into madness, ("O what a noble mind is here o'erthrown").

First one frames the simplest and most accurate action-lines that one can; that is those charged sentences which contain the essence of the characters' deepest intentions.

HAMLET	OPHELIA
I want to demonstrate my madness	I want you to be the person I used to love

HAMLET	OPHELIA
I want to punish you for plotting against me.	I don't want to get hurt.
I want to destroy all women.	I want to survive this encounter.
I want everyone to see how dangerous I can be.	I want to show my father and the king I am an innocent victim of circumstances . . ..

Once the action-lines have been agreed upon by the actors - the scene is replayed with the original blocking using only the action-lines or slight variations of same. The original text is forbidden the actors.

Once this has been done, the actors are encouraged to choose three or four key-words that they believe contain the essence of the actions; (e. g. "madness," "be love," "punish," "hurt," "destroy," "survive, etc."). These words are extracted from the action-lines. The scene is then played again using only those key-words.

This done, the actors are asked to construct a sound drawn from the vowels and consonants of the key-words and to explore the deepest, most animalistic impulses of the scene, still loosely within the physical framework of the scene as prepared.

In this final replay, all conventional staging is abandoned and the actors are encouraged to express, in unfettered physical terms, whatever emotions are released by the confrontation.

Finally, the scene is reassembled and played straight.

If the progression from simple sentences to key-words to sounds has worked properly, the actors will have experienced a conflict in the scene above and beyond the one depicted in the text. For in this 'straightforward' scene, apart from Hamlet demonstrating his distraction to the King and Polonius and deliberately abusing Ophelia, there is an unconscious animus between the prince and his courtly girlfriend nourished by an ambivalence towards his mother, a frustrated hatred for Claudius, and a bristling contempt for his own impotence in being denied the kingship to which he is rightfully entitled. This is further complicated by the knowledge of his mother's incest and the awareness that he has let down all those in the kingdom who have eagerly waited for him to ascend the throne.

From Ophelia's standpoint, there is a steaming stew of mixed emotions. She must painfully reassess the Prince's feelings for her and vice versa. She must adapt herself to the knowledge that she is now at the center of a political intrigue which puts her father in one camp and the Prince in the other. Then there are questions of personal safety mingled with implications of impropriety for having originally yielded to Hamlet's advances which, in the new dispensation, may be misconstrued as disloyalty to the new sovereign. Whatever affection she may have had for the Prince, it may now be politic to deny it - even if it runs counter to her true feelings. Also to be taken into account is her complicity in her father's stratagem and the fact that her own sexuality, which on the basis of later evidence is formidable, must now, in the light of the new political dispensation, be rigorously curbed.

As if that were not enough, there is also Hamlet's profound disgust with the frailty of women and the corruption in a society which is the antithesis of the world idealized in his studies at Wittenberg and which, being young and idealistic, may well incline him towards both cynicism and despair.

Every time Hamlet is on stage, no matter what the scene, he contains in himself a multitude of ambivalent feelings which are as much part of his temperament as those that may be activated by any one given set of circumstances. So it is never a matter of going piecemeal into the scenes of the play but bearing in mind that the character is himself a totality of sensations, impulses and attitudes and though, at any given time, one emotion may take precedence over another, there is never a moment when the whole galaxy of his feelings do not interact together.

If that is the case, how simplistic and inadequate it would be to settle for, and try to achieve, one clear-cut 'objective' for, as in life, there is never a single objective which isn't conjoined with dozens of others, pulling people into several directions at once.

*   *   *   *   *

The underlying aim of rehearsals is for the actor to accumulate as much relevant experience as possible. The deeper he digs his well, the more he has to draw on when the time comes to sustain his performance during a run. The problem with most rehearsal periods is that, due to the limitations of time and the miscalculation of priorities, the actor seeks only to *parallel* his role or *roughly approximate* the emotional graph of his character. 'Getting beneath the skin' of his role is a common objective; penetrating its soul is not.

According to Method doctrines, there is a tacit assumption that if the actor can color the character with his own feelings, create a viable 'identification,' that correspondence will see him through. The idea that he may be obliged to discover an inner core radically different from his own, and consequently much less accessible to emotional approximations, rarely occurs to him. As a result, most performances merely point up the disparity between the size and scope of the play's intentions and the meagreness of the actor trying to achieve them. It is the shallowness of the actor's rehearsal experience, the modesty of his goals, which accounts for this artistic malnutrition. If the most the actor is expected to deliver is assimilation of text and a rough indication of sub-text, why should anyone expect a resonating or far-reaching performance that brings new and greater dimension to the playwright's work? Having drilled only a matter of inches beneath the surface of his role, the actor merely recycles his paltry findings from one performance to the next and then complains bitterly about the boredom and monotony of his profession, desperately seeking the stimulus of a new role, a new play, a new experience from which he hopes to derive greater satisfaction - never realizing that it is his own shallowness which is responsible for his frustration. It is the variety and intensity of the actor's rehearsal experience which determines the breadth and weight of what he creates. The more he ventures, the more he gains; the further he travels through the labyrinth of his private world and then back again, the more he has to report back to his public.

*   *   *   *

According to the Stanislavskyian canon, all roles can be reduced to motive and objective. The character has 'wants' and in order to satisfy them, he constructs a sequence of actions to achieve that aim. It is a conception of human nature as simplistic as the 19th century philosophy which informed it; a conception that denies or ignores the multiplicity of human psychology and the fact that the a character's 'wants' are often contradictory, lateral to his consciousness and frequently the opposite of what he declares them to be. Subtext, in the Stanislavskyian dispensation, becomes the lock into which the key neatly fits, but for every door it opens, ten others remain inaccessible. Ur-text is like the master-key that opens all doors - because it denies the notion that one key fits only one lock. It infers that there are many keys and many locks and, at the same time, declares that even when *all* doors have been unlocked, there are hidden corridors, underground tunnels and sliding panels above and beyond the orderly rooms that make up the mansion.

Let's look for a moment at this notion of multiplicity as it operates in our own lives and then in the actor creating his role.

An actor 'making a choice' necessarily rejects other possibilities which have presented themselves for consideration. In opting for one action over another, he denies himself the residues which cling to alternative or counter-desires. For example, when we step into the bank-president's office to request a loan, one part of us is confident that our proposal is sound and deserves approval, another is steeled for defeat; a third feels we are outrageous impostors trying to obtain money under false pretenses; a fourth envies the resources of an institution which, if there were justice in the world, would be as much *our* resources as they are the bank's; a fifth may be suppressing an overwhelming sense of worthlessness based on past financial failures which are resolutely suppressed; a sixth may be hoping for rejection so that a great gamble need never be undertaken and an easy rationalization provided for its abandonment; a seventh may be smoldering with irrational contempt for being obliged to come begging for money in the first place.

What is the sub-text of such a scene? It's like asking how many layers are there in an onion? How many grooves make up a pineapple?

Before opting for one choice over another, it is useful to feel the multiplicity of emotions that swirl beneath such a scene, so that alternative or contradictory choices can be 'experienced' before being merged into the scene-proper.

Before the scene between the client and the bank-manager is played out, several actors in an improvisation are assigned the 'roles' of the client's alter-egos - those sides of him which represent the many facets of the scene's latent content. One is assigned the part of him consumed by envy, another the side of him anticipating defeat; another, the side of him which feels utterly worthless, etc., etc. The alter-egos are clustered around the client and they react to the bank-manager at the same time the client does - although exclusively in terms of their own emotional strand. When the client responds in what seems to him to be appropriate behavior, each alter-ego responds simultaneously from their own standpoint. This will produce a clatter of voices all sounding at once but, despite the fact that there may be seven or eight characters radiating from the client, each will be reacting in accordance with his prescribed quality. When the client moves during the scene, his cluster of alter-egos moves with him. When he sits, they do likewise. At all times, the group-reactions are triggered by the other character (i.e., the bank-manager) as if they possessed independent existences - however, they are physically and rhythmically tied to the client and can only respond when he does, and it is important at all times clearly to stress their relation to the main character.

If this exercise is performed correctly, the client experiences a jumble of mixed emotions, one for each of the alter-egos in the scene. Some may fortify his own responses; some may contradict them. He may, because of certain sentiments expressed by his alter-egos, become aware of certain incongruities in his responses to the bank manager, certain attitudes antithetical to those he is expressing. At first, he may be confused, but as he proceeds to play the scene *a deux*, some of the remnants from the exercise will cling to his performance; a residue of other feelings inspired by traits with which he may not agree but which he cannot ignore. Ultimately, his own performance will acquire more nuance, more color, more complexity than was the case before he admitted his alter-egos, and sub-text will have given way to something far more potent beneath it.

*   *   *   *   *

We talk loosely and rather imprecisely about a stratum of experience beyond the psychological. Although it defies exact description, we are all aware of it. While it is more easily traceable in animals, it is reasonable to assume that at some earlier stage of our development, these same instincts existed in us - and in some blurred and ineffable way still do. Bees, for instance, have an unerring sense of direction as do certain species of birds which migrate and return from migration almost as if they had a compass. We know that animals (from the lion to the cockroach) have certain hidden antennae that alert them to danger. Once upon a time, our own sense of smell was as highly developed as canines'. We too, in our prehistoric past, could sniff out food, locate shelter, seek out protection against attack.

Our herd instincts are not at all extinct. We still find them emerging when we hear of instances of gang-rape, outbreaks of hooliganism during spring breaks, or collective fervor at political rallies and sports events. The gangs in downtown Los Angeles and other urban ghettos remind us that we still hunt in packs, that we are still motivated by vengeance, that our young still prove their manhood through ritualistic acts of violence.

Language is a relatively recent development. Before we refined a means of communication that relied on words and signals, we employed inflections and intonations, cries and grunts, a vast vocabulary of sounds which expressed the wide range of emotions for which we later developed a subtle terminology. Certain scientists believe that the movements of our tongues merely imitate the primitive actions that preceded the formulation of speech. What we call telepathy may simply be the vestiges of sense-perceptions that existed before the advent of spoken language; not *super* sensory but *sub*-sensuous phenomena.

The analysts tell us that the child is buried inside the man; the anthropologist that the tribal instinct still flickers behind the facades of modern civilization. We, at the threshold of the new millennium, are not the furthest point of history's development, we *are* history. We contain it as assuredly as the streets of Europe contain the epochs of previous civilizations buried beneath its stones.

When we feel frightened or threatened, fervent or cowed, passionate or revolted, the socialized expression of all these states winds downward into emotional caverns which have never been permanently sealed off. And it is by making the connections between the roots of these feelings and their surface representation that we bring to the theatre something more than simulacra.

*   *   *   *

The greatest barrier to the actor's exploration is language; the literalness of the author's text which appears to legislate one reality and no other. And yet all language undergoes a transformation when it is placed in the mouths of actors and conditioned by their sensibility. The whole notion of sub-text - the fact that it is a qualification of language (sub *text*) indicates the timorousness with which the Stanislavsky-actor approaches the playwright's work. The actor has to realize that language, as Artaud said, is only "the stitch of thought" and that it is the actor's responsibility to create the psychic conditions which justifies the words the playwright has put into his mouth. To do this, he has to situate himself as far away from text as the author himself did before he ever put pen to paper. It is by creating a parallel journey from impulse to speech that the actor is able to fulfill the tacit contract he has undertaken with the playwright - viz. not merely to speak his words but to recreate the emotional network to which they correspond.

Strictly speaking, Ur-text is not textual at all. Fundamentally, the term is a misnomer for a potentiality that has no clear-cut terms. Freud wanting to label an essential quality of our nature beyond the grasp of visible behavior, came up with the term *das est* which in English was translated as the id. Ur-text is just as quintessential, just as elusive and indefinable. It almost doesn't matter what one calls it so long as one distinguishes it from the visible, tangible, measurable trait the actor constructs as part of his social and psychological make-up. What is important is the realization that whatever this quality is, it transcends psychological motivation and supersedes deductive logic. Just as at the root of all science and physics there lies an impenetrable mystery which science and physics attempt to elucidate through coded intelligence, so there is an underlying truth behind all actions and objectives which cannot be captured by a systematizing consciousness. And since it lurks precisely in those areas furthest from the conscious mind, it is through lateral thought and unconscious stratagems that we must seek out its mysteries.

*   *   *   *

THE ART OF PROVOCATION

The underlying purpose of rehearsals is to prod the actor's imagination into areas relevant to the given material. Yet the irresistible tendency of rehearsals is to routinize and deaden the imagination because time is so often taken up with mechanical procedures such as fixing moves and learning lines. In every rehearsal period, these two impulses - the imaginative and the routine - are continually in conflict and the success of any production depends on whether imagination or automatism gains the upper hand.

Every moment spent in releasing a play needs to have a clear-cut or intuited objective. A rehearsal without a specific problem to solve necessarily dwindles into the automatic assembly of its technical parts. What should be sculpture becomes bricklaying. A brief description of the scene's aim, its raison-d'etre and its relevance to the scenes that surround it, serves to provide actors with both a framework and a goal. It reinforces the fact, so easily lost in the self-absorption of rehearsals, that all the players, despite the variety of their goals, have a common purpose. Sometimes a generalized description of the needs of a scene will unearth the specific motivations upon which its overall dramatic charge depends. In by-passing the actions of individual characters and concentrating instead on the requirement of the scene, that is, in generalizing the dramatic situation instead of particularizing each actor's part in it, the imagination of the entire company gets harnessed to a collective aim. The director, at such times, is like a football coach laying out a game-plan which individual players will interpret for themselves once they take the field.

Method actors tend to recoil from any attempt to pry them out of their personal shells. I have known Method actors refuse to discuss the strategy of a scene with their fellow-actor because it would interfere with the assembly of their own personal actions. The assumption of such actors is: I must find the truth (i.e., point and purpose) of my own activity in the scene - and you must find *yours* - only then can we make organic connections with one another.

The truth of a scene - just as the truth of an entire play - cannot be separated from the contiguity of its whole. A rigorously subjective Stanislavsky approach may pay lip-service to contact, but it cannot help but sever the fine tissue that needs to spring up among all the members of a company. While an actor is selfishly immersed in the complexities of his personal action, it is easy to overlook the objective of the overall scene. An actor may be delving into the personal truth of *his* actions, while he unwittingly forfeits or reverses the author's objective. Method actors lose sight of the fact that the playwright *also* has 'actions' and 'objectives' and that unless a character's aim gibes with the play's aim it cannot be legitimate - no matter how striking its dramatic effect.

What the Method has done over the past fifty years is to shift the balance of power away from the playwright and towards the actor. Whereas this has produced some startling performance results, it has revealed an alarming tendency to subvert the integrity of the play - whether a new work or a classic - although it is more apparent in classics where a uniformity - of - style is demanded and personal idiosyncrasy more conspicuous.

The actor warms up. He limbers his body; he tries to eliminate all muscular tensions. He does vocal exercises to "free up" his voice, to increase his resonance, to make his diction more precise. In short, he attempts to make his physical organism as responsive as possible to his creativity. But no sooner do rehearsals begin than he finds himself 'setting moments,' deciding on inflections and reactions in order to 'fix' them into the growing tapestry which is his role. All the time laboriously spent in lubricating his imagination for a free and unfettered rehearsal is squandered in the automatism of a dry practice session. Again, the sculptor has given way to the bricklayer.

The actor, like the character, needs to be *provoked* into behavior and to achieve this, an element of surprise is necessary. It is the actor's awareness of his scene's futurity - what is coming up just around the corner - that robs him of freshness and spontaneity; that leads him into faking the experience of 'the first time.' The paradox of the actor is that he is asked to play in the present tense, moment to moment, while having already worked out a detailed road-map of the future.

The character knows nothing of the future. He may have anticipations, indications, even clear presentiments of what the future will hold, but cannot say precisely what will happen, in what order or with what intensity. The actor, on the other hand, knows it all but must pretend that he knows nothing; that he is living 'in the moment' and going from 'moment to moment'. As a result, he frequently anticipates, signals the moments to come, is mechanical, where he should be open, venturesome, unaware. He becomes predictable and his predictability robs him of plausibility. We, the audience, know that the actor knows precisely what lies ahead and so when it comes, it is as unsurprising to us as it is to him. The contemporary audience through constant exposure to films, television, novels and plays, has become so sophisticated that it is already one jump ahead of the actor and this foreknowledge of events dissipates its interest as the play unfolds.

But every play production is predicated on precisely this kind of organization of future events. A 'rehearsal' means a repetition of lines and moves in order to 'get them right,' make them a credible forerunner to what is to come. How then can we live in the present if our minds and our biologies are constantly anticipating the future? We cannot pretend *not* to know something when we know it.

Acting is not the art of repetition, it is the art of provocation - being simultaneously stirred by internal impulses and external events. The actor, in order to 'rehearse' those parts of himself most vital to the process, must experience incitement to thought and instigation to action. To achieve this, the director must constantly surprise the actor by reorganizing the stimuli he encounters in the scene. This can sometimes be achieved by issuing covert instructions to the actor's playing-partners thereby altering or reversing the gist of their behavior - consciously re-angling the details of their actions so as to elicit different ones. This needs to be done arbitrarily, illogically, unjustifiably - producing a reaction which the actor realizes is wrong, *not in keeping* with what has come before, incongruous to the situation. The wrongness of all these mini-events will succeed in breaking the mold that is too rapidly set in the actor's work. Once the 'mistakes' have been experienced, it is easy to discard them - to return to the logic of the scene and the consistency of the characters' behavior - but the 'mistake,' the anomaly, the choice 'from left field' has immense value in itself - as it is accidents and unforeseen events which alienate (i.e., in the Brechtian sense of casting in a new light) the normality which has come to be taken for granted.

We open the front door and discover it is actually a closet-door; it refreshes our understanding of what a front-door is. We expect a kiss from our sweetheart and instead we get a slap in the face. We rebel at the 'unexpectedness,' but we learn to appreciate the fact that we have routinely come to expect it. The moment is no longer a *fait-accompli* . In a very literal sense, a play is made up of a series of *fait-accomplis* disguised as a natural sequence of unfolding events. When the actor rethinks the *fait-accompli* he may understand why the original event was inevitable and irreversible and took the precise form it did.

The actor walks into a room expecting to find his wife in the arms of her discarded male lover; instead, she is being kissed and fondled by the maid. Outrageous, and unaccountable behavior! Is this wife a lesbian? Does she have tendencies towards her own sex? Probably not; more likely than not there are no such inferences in the play - but during the split-second when she is discovered in a flagrantly uncharacteristic embrace, the nature of her *characteristic* behavior is reaffirmed.

Horatio cradles the dead prince in his arms. Inside, he is welling up with rage and confusion, impotence and loss. Suddenly, the prince stirs. "No, no, you're dead; lie down; let me get out my lines." Let the play run its proper course. The sudden restoration of Hamlet's life is totally insupportable, but might it clarify the jumble of emotions going on in Horatio's mind? Might it define which of those mixed emotions should be primary? What effect would such a reincarnation have on Fortinbras who is already looking around the corpse-strewn chamber contemplating how he will redecorate Elsinore and install his own people.

This fanciful, quirky rehearsal experiment may give the actor a sense of the unresolved immediacy of Hamlet's death. If it prevents him from playing the past-tense rather than the present, of avoiding the cliché of the new leader rising out of the dead ashes of the old one, it may well serve a purpose. Anything that cracks the mosaic of preordained circumstances is worth trying.

All true action is provoked into being. We only examine a character's motivation after the fact in order to determine the reasons he or she was provoked into action. Initially, it is the provocation, which triggers the event. In our own lives, the most dramatic events are those which are neither premeditated nor entirely understood. After a progressive series of frustrations, something snaps and we throw a plate at the mirror or a book at the head of a loved one. The impulse to action, the provocation to express our feeling, is unrehearsed; it takes us by surprise.

This is just as true about spoken revelations whether they be professions of love or the release of pent-up enmity. Something takes hold of us and the next thing we know we are doing and saying things that are unexpected and astonish ourselves and those around us. All 'dramatic action' no matter how studiously contemplated, happens in that split-second when interior forces ignite external action. But the routinization of rehearsals trammel up the 'cue to action;' it intellectualizes what should be instinctive and regulates what should be spontaneous. The more the actor can experience unexpected provocations, the more he makes contact with the lifeblood of his character's inner life; the very force that tends to get labeled and codified in rehearsals.

Cassius confronts Brutus in the Tent Scene to demand an explanation for his partner's unfriendly behavior in the war. Play it with a shield in front of your face rendering Brutus invisible, forcing only his words to convey his feelings. Immediately, the overweening desire for contact between the two characters is abruptly frustrated. As a result, Cassius must, with greater concentration, try to discern the subtleties of Brutus' explanations. Being unable to read his facial changes, Cassius must try all the harder to interpret the subtextual meanings behind Brutus' words. He is obliged to listen much more intently since he is dealing only with Brutus' voice. There's less chance of him becoming inured to Brutus' defensiveness, hostility and melancholia.

Romeo, after lyrically expressing his feelings, climbs up the balcony to embrace Juliet only to discover the Nurse has been privy to all his protestations. How does he proceed in the face of this unexpected intrusion? How does Juliet? What does the removal of this 'third party' tell the actors about the quality of their privacy when they *are* alone? Irrelevant and unwarranted intrusions into Shakespeare's scene which, when eliminated, heighten the reality of the scene itself.

The Method actor is taught that in order to create dramatic tension, an obstacle needs to be placed in a scene which must then be negotiated. Usually, that obstacle is an intellectual choice made by the actor often in consultation with the director. But sometimes to provoke the actor into fresh activity, it is useful for the obstacle to be tangible.

Claudius, in order to manipulate Laertes for his own ends, devises

a plot whereby Hamlet may be poisoned in a duel. Laertes, still mourn-
ing the unexpected death of his father, tries to balance his sense of loss
and his desire for revenge. Instead of two characters facing each other
at opposite ends of a table, the actors have a long rope wound around
their waists. As Claudius draws Laertes into his web, he tugs the rope
pulling Laertes towards him. As Laertes experiences misgivings about
Claudius' motives, he winds himself away from the King. As the King's
arguments take on greater force, Claudius draws Laertes closer to him,
tangling the rope around him like a cowboy roping a young calf.
Laertes yields to the King, letting his own rope drop from his hands, allowing himself to be wound up in the King's.

By means of the rope, the subtle subtextual tugs that condition the
scene are visibly played out; the 'obstacle' of the rope operates like a
graph revealing how one character persuades and manipulates, how the
other ruminates and tries to elude, or yields and succumbs to the other's
demands.

Afterwards, the director may question *this* tug or *that* pull. Does
Claudius really draw Laertes in at that point, or is he really twirling the
rope nonchalantly before tightening it into a noose? The rope trick
provides the means to gauge each actor's detailed judgment in regard to
each line, each speech, each emotional permutation of the scene. It is
a scan of the play's biology that can pinpoint the problem areas.

Just as the actor is discouraged from 'playing results' (arbitrarily
jumping to emotional conclusions), so the director must be dissuaded
from verbally dramatizing the effects he would like to achieve. The
rhetorical description of a desired climax or the lyrical conjuration of a
certain atmosphere is usually an eloquent waste of time. Just as the

actor resists line readings from his director, so he tacitly resents the director's 'performance' of effects he would like him to achieve. The director is not there to evoke, in high-sounding words and histrionic demonstrations, the qualities and attitudes he would like his actors to engender, but to devise methodical means - exercises, activities, and re-hearsal-tactics - which will coax them into being. The caricature of the silent film director emoting the scene for the mesmerized actor who will subsequently mimic his prescribed gestures and facial expressions has unfortunately been replaced by the stage-director who feels he or she can produce an acting result by means of animated and dramatic verbal dissertations. Both belong to a bygone era.

Just as there is a life force in rehearsals, there is also a death instinct; a tendency to suck the blood out of living moments by treating them like so much inanimate matter. The good director fosters that life force; the bad one, succumbs to Thanatos.

Behind the text of any play, there are more motions than can ever surface into the scene, but the more of them that can be activated, the richer its texture will be. The further away certain choices are from those which are apparently relevant to the given situation, the more information the actor brings to bear on his overall conception of the play; the more pastel shades there are to supplement his primary colors. But in order for the scene to grow living tissue, the actor has to be physically stimulated into action. It is by being provoked into action that he gets stimulated into thought. Too often, the process is reversed. Actors theorize rather than experience behavior, intellectually select the shortest route between two points and unwaveringly follow it. There may be a treasure of new revelations found on the road not taken.

It has been said that the best way to experience an unfamiliar city is to get lost in its winding thoroughfares. In acting, the carefully guided tour that lingers at all the most familiar sites can sometimes be the very thing which prevents discovery.

*   *   *   *

THE ACTOR'S PROBLEM

You say you're having problems?

I am feeling paralyzed. I've been rehearsing this role for over three weeks now and feel I am getting nowhere. I've tried to work up parallel experience, find some actual character on which to base my portrayal. I worked up emotional-memories based on incidents when I was jealous or covetous or treacherous, but Macbeth just eludes me.

You say you've explored 'parallel experience.' Have you ever contemplated the murder of a supreme authority such as a king or a president?

Of course not.

Then what kind of parallel experience do you have for a man who plans the murder of one who rules by divine right?

I wanted to be class president once and a good friend of mine was chosen instead; I wanted to be valedictorian at my graduation, but it never happened.

Are those 'parallel' experiences to Macbeth?

Well, not really, I guess.

Not only are they not parallel, they are drawing you away from the world of the play. "Macbeth" has nothing to do with your college frustrations or your longings for minor distinctions. This is a man who is being tempted into an act of regicide; a crime which will transform him and his society utterly and affect an entire political realm. How can mundane naturalistic experience from your past ever hope to condition the motives of such a person?

But I was taught to use my own experience in building a character - to draw on things that I know.

The most significant knowledge that you have is the play - its text and reverberations. You can see at a glance that the world depicted in that play, is radically different from your own. The play is an imaginative construct. Shakespeare never murdered a king; was not married to a scheming, ambitious wife who coaxed him into committing a heinous political crime. In trying to realize his play, you are being invited into an imaginative world much more charged and specialized than that of your limited experience. What makes you think you can unlock a castle door with a flimsy little postbox key?

But my own personal experience is all I have. My personalized knowledge of ambition and desire, of jealousy and conspiracy.

What makes you think that your imaginative capabilities are in some way inferior to your actual experience? What makes you believe that you cannot conjure up, as an artist on the stage the world that Shakespeare has conjured up as an artist on the page?

Are you saying that I'm not capable of such a role?

On the contrary. I'm saying you're entirely capable - but only if you meet Shakespeare on his own terms - in his own sphere - and that sphere is the poetic imagination. Personally you've never contemplated murder or been harried by witches - but examine your dreams and you'll discover that you've been enmeshed in terrible crimes and have known the prodding of demons. On an imaginary level you have already undergone many of the emotions that beset Macbeth. Everything that happens in that play is part of a terrible nightmare. Macbeth is an insomniac; he tells us over and over again how hard it is for him to sleep; to distinguish between the real world and the world of his tortured imagination. So you see, you do have a powerful parallel experience: your dream-life.

But I have to rehearse this role in the waking world - not when I'm asleep.

And you will when you've conjured up that 'dream world' in your waking world. The two worlds constantly interact in Macbeth's mind. By launching your imagination into the teeming imagination of the work, you are meeting Shakespeare on his own terms. You are not merely reducing a great classic to a pedestrian and prosaic experience - something in keeping with the scale of your own naturalistic experience - but exploring it in that area of your imagination that corresponds to that of the author's.

Yes, okay, but how?

The answers to that question are endless. They depend on exercises, improvisations and suppositions that have to be made in every scene of the play; ways of researching feelings that delve beyond the simplistic level of psychology; assaults on language and sound, movement and action which move far beyond verisimilitude. Every actor has some quotient of metaphysics in his nature and they would discover it if only they went further than the epidermal search for psychology.

I was taught that the most important resource I had as an actor was myself. That bad acting consisted of forgetting myself - adopting external characteristics - instead of incorporating what was essentially my own being, my own mind, my own talent.

But how would it ever be possible to disengage yourself from these things? Your body, your mind, your intellect, your Self - these things are always and inescapably part of you. But a body that does not adapt to the chemistry of your character; a mind that stays moored to irrelevant, naturalistic concerns, an intellect that doesn't transcend the obvious, and a notion of selfhood that prevents you from transforming yourself into something greater than yourself, - what does all that do but demean your talent? What you have been taught is to retreat to your own limited boundaries, but when you approach a great classical role - or any truly complex part - you are obliged to extend your self - to become more than you were before - to achieve new heights and greater depths. The sure way of avoiding that challenge is to aggrandize your 'self' as if you, in your limited sphere of social experience, were quite sufficient to cope with any task placed before it.

The actor is in a chronic state of repetition. He standardizes what he has done before; reproduces what has served him in the past, and all for very good reason. He has proven to himself that what he has done before works. It achieves results. It elicits praise. It creates new employment opportunities. Why shouldn't he reheat old effects; recycle previous successes?

Well, the reason is that no two roles are the same. Each new role, particularly the more challenging ones, imposes different demands on his resources. But because he is a creature of habit, a robot of repetition, he has automatized himself - turned his demonstrable assets into a mechanism which eventually becomes second nature. But there's really no such thing as *second nature;* there is only Nature - variegated and unique - always fresh, always adaptive, always in a state of flux. The actor's past success may prove the greatest obstacle to his future if he prizes the finished article rather than the marvelous machinery that can be adapted to create any article he wishes.

We disdain those actors who are continually type-cast, but what *is* a typecast actor but one who has solidified habits of speech and behavior so that they can be reproduced on demand. They have converted their talent into commodities and because the theatre is a business and commodities are prized by businesses, they regularly market their wares. They are as familiar as a brand-name; as a box of cereal that always contains the same texture or a soft drink that always has the same flavor. But don't mistake them for creative artists because creativity shuns that kind of predictable uniformity. Creativity, because it never quite knows where it is going and is not afraid to launch itself into uncharted waters, lives dangerously and makes discoveries. The commodity-actor is what the creative actor turns into once he has accepted the limitations of his Self. Yes, he is 'playing himself' all right, but what a mingy, poverty-stricken self it is. The sin is not playing oneself but not having enough of oneself to play.

What are rehearsals for? If all our rehearsals accomplish is setting lines and moves and fixing the progressive action of the play, all we're doing is building a house out of cardboard. The first strong wind that comes along will blow it over.

A rehearsal is an opportunity to 'find something' - to have an experience - to collide with another actor, a notion, a suspicion, a paradox, a secret, a revelation. There is nothing quite so tedious as the work of a gold-prospector - constantly panning dirt and water in search of gold dust. But the gold prospector doesn't find it tedious because he knows that in every pan of water and handful of dirt, a treasure may be discovered. The same is true of the archeologist who digs and sifts and digs again. Behind all that routine digging and sifting, the critical intelligence is analyzing and probing, always hopeful that the next shovel will hit metal or a piece of precious ceramic.

The actor who uses rehearsals to solidify matter which has not yet been sifted and tested is, metaphorically speaking, burying himself. A true discovery - whether it be an inflection or a move, a nuance or a pause, can only come about if the magnetic field of the play has been unearthed. Like the archeologist's treasure or the miner's gold dust, there has to be a kind of heightened anticipation of what is being sought and a sensitivity as to when, and under what circumstances, it can be found. This means probing and testing, sifting and assessing - not 'setting' and 'fixing.'

A healthy rehearsal is one in which an actor, or a director or dramaturg, suddenly asks a question which cannot be answered by reference to the given material - forcing everyone to reassess all that has gone before. To return to the goldminer's analogy, if the dig has been started on the wrong site, it may make more sense to start again in a more potential place than to dig deeper and deeper into empty bedrock. The actor's divining-rod must always be in front of him' he must respond to its every fluctuation. If that means agonizing reappraisal of previous choices and prior assumptions, that is all to the good. Sometimes the smallest discovery in the most minor scene produces the key to a wholesale reinterpretation of the entire play. But that can only happen if lines and moves, gestures and intonations, texts and pretexts are tentative and the actor vigilant - constantly affirming or rejecting the discovery of each succeeding moment.

Skepticism is the actor's most valuable rehearsal tool because it prevents the complacency which comes with self-indulgence and the fallacies which become inbred through the customary way of working.

But once the actor has found his way, tested his choices, decided on his tactics, mustn't rehearsals batten down the hatches? Mustn't the performance get solidified?

Only the presence of the audience can 'solidify' the performance. The task of rehearsals is to methodically create the runway which allows the performance to take off - for clearly, until the audience is there, the most crucial dimension is not yet in place.

But surely, the purpose of the rehearsal period is to create a finished article for the sake of the audience. If the process is to go on beyond dress-rehearsals, beyond previews, beyond the opening, that makes a mockery of the entire process of preparing a play.

But nothing you do can prevent it from going on. Once a mise-en-scene meets an audience, it dynamically adjusts itself. Some things fall away - some things solidify - some things are helplessly thrown into question. An opening night performance is a social event, not an artistic resolution. That is why the rehearsal-period has to be thought of as a methodical preparation for an existential event - the event being the artifact functioning in *different publics* - as many as there are performances. Throughout this ongoing process, the performance is refining propositions on which it has been based. That is why the actor must realize that the final stroke, the final surrender can never be made during the rehearsal period. That is why his greatest energy, his greatest daring, must be kept in reserve for the final phase - which isn't the dress rehearsal or the preview but the first weeks of the run. The time when the artist and the public experience the spontaneous combustion which either proves or disproves the assumptions of all the preceding weeks.

But if that's the case, what's to prevent the whole show from transforming entirely after it opens?

Nothing, and it often does. What is more likely is that various portions of it are accepted or rejected - prove viable or non-viable - and, depending on which proportion is greater, it succeeds or fails. But from the actor's standpoint, it is immediately after the opening that his performance makes that final ascent into resolved experience. It is in the atmosphere conditioned by a living public that the actor does his most crucial work, makes his most valuable discoveries, finally confirms the true path into his role.

Everything you seem to be saying runs contrary to what I and other actors have been taught - that finding and playing one's objective is what is primary - that the actor's job is to simulate reality - to try to create fictions that the audience will believe in; that the actor's task is to suspend the disbelief of the audience.

Of course actions have to be found, sub-text explored, reality simulated, suspension of disbelief maintained. From ancient Greece to the present, these have been the aims of acting and the principles behind stagecraft. But these things are no longer sufficient. Over the past one hundred and fifty years, acting-theory has ossified into shibboleths and catch phrases. The revolution begun by Andre Antoine and Konstantin Stanislavsky has been superseded by new events, new technologies, new innovations in style and content. No revolutionary movement can stand still for a century and expect that it is still moving with the times.

Psychological realism reached a kind of apogee in the 50s with Miller and Williams, Inge and others of that school. Although David Mamet and Harold Pinter seem to be writing in the same vein, the fact is their 'realism' is far less 'psychological,' far more 'mystical' and chameleon. The new content - that is the new preoccupations of the new millennium - are pushing playwrights, directors and designers onto new turf. Not only is their subject-matter different, their mode of perception has changed - influenced, as it has been, by modern technology, changing values and a post modernist caste-of-mind. Not only do people believe different things today, they actively *disbelieve* things they were taught by previous generations. There is a new skepticism, if not wholesale denial, of the ideas that were rife only fifty or seventy-five years ago. There is a distrust of ideals and idealists; of political leaders and political platforms; a suspicion of lawyers and doctors, advertising men and religious leaders - of all those vacuous truths that the media is constantly hammering into the public on the false assumption that they are being uncritically accepted. A new coarseness has entered into personal relations - a more practical, cold-blooded approach to courtship and marriage, the role of women - in regard to both men and property - to careers and home-making. And concurrent with all these changes, a new way of interacting with one another and with the larger beliefs that now influence society.

All of these things have happened while actors have continued to pay lip-service to the old platitudes. In every age, it is the plays that condition the actors; the sensibility of the new writers that determine the nature of the performance. It was Hugo that brought romanticism into being - just as it was Ibsen and Chekhov that perfected social realism as a prevailing style; just as it was Miller and Williams who transformed it into something more psychological and more poetic. The artifacts condition the performers who perform them and today, we have a theatre infiltrated by impulses from MTV and Performance Art, assimilating the influences of writers as dissimilar as Jean Genet and Bertolt Brecht, theorists as far removed from one another as Marshall McLuhan and Michael Foucault.

Don't tell me that a sensibility invaded by influences as diverse as these can be regulated by the esthetic principles hammered out at the turn of the century. They can't. A new dispensation is afoot - but the actor, weaned on the techniques of naturalism and realism, Cocteau and Sartre, Brecht and Artaud, cannot assimilate these new influences unless they bend and adapt, jettison what no longer applies and bring new techniques and new means of expression into what is an entirely new equation.

By religiously applying doctrines and techniques which no longer serve our immediate needs, we are moving in ever-diminishing circles. To progress necessarily means replacing methods and ideas which have lost their currency. If the world is truly more complex and more unpredictable, driven by different priorities, responsive to different ideas and motivated by a set of ideologies that reorder our value-system, the actor has to absorb these differences in order to express them. That change-of-sensibility is not restricted to the new work, but to the way in which contemporary artists regard the old work. Classics need to be radically reconsidered - *are* being radically reconsidered because they are the repositories of the traditional beliefs which we are rapidly revising or discarding.

All of that may be true, but none of it is helping me with my 'Macbeth.'

Quite right, when you come right down to it, a handful of practical suggestions are worth a ton of polemics.

All right, let's take a look at his first entrance. A soldier, weary from battle and in the company of an officer every bit as courageous as himself, stumbles upon three old hags who announce that he will take on the title of a nobleman (whom he believes to be still alive) and shortly after that, become the supreme ruler of the realm. Is this a witch's prophecy or the projection of the soldier's secret burning desire - and why is his comrade privy to it? Is it because his fate is already sealed as well? Do people like Banquo and Macbeth *make* their fate or encounter it from without? - What are they both doing on that heath anyway? - What sort of illusions are battle-weary soldiers prone to? Does battle-fatigue bring on hallucinations? Are there witches there at all? Are they actually on a heath? Is Banquo Banquo? or a fearful projection of Macbeth's chief rival in the inevitable struggle for advancement which follows an insurrection?

Now you're talking!

On the contrary - now I'm just restating the obvious. Talking is what we were doing a moment ago.

"Hamlet" (Adapted by Marowitz) Anthony Haygarth. Open Space Theatre, 1975

Donald Cooper Photography

*   *   *   *

UNMASKING THE MASKED ACTOR

The auditioning actor is there to demonstrate the range of his skills and the competence of his technique. He is putting on a show and the purpose of that show is to display his talents. It usually takes the form of a monologue, comic or straight, which has been studiously committed to memory and delivered so many times before it has now become ingrained. Through the recurring rituals of audition, the actor's face has become a mask.

The actor is auditioning because he is looking for work. The director is looking for other things. He wants to garner information about the actor's personality as well as his grasp of technique. He also wants to know whether the actor is capable of variety and change, susceptible to direction and able to express more depth than is usually apparent in a short audition. He is also concerned with certain marginal social issues. Is the actor amenable or obnoxious? Does he have sufficient intellect to grasp an idea as well as technical directions? Is he disruptive or cooperative, a good team-player or a rampaging individualist? Although he can immediately recognize skill, he wonders if the skill has scope. Is what he sees all he is going to get?

Of course, none of these questions can be answered during a conventional audition since the actor is masked and the director has neither the gumption nor the right to question him directly, and even if he did, he would not receive informative answers. A disruptive or obnoxious actor never recognizes these traits in himself; a shallow actor, even if he senses that his lack of depth will never admit it in a potential employment situation. A conventional job-applicant may fill out a questionnaire and undergo a battery of interviews, but all an actor can do is flash his mask.

The director can learn almost nothing from an audition-piece which has congealed from years of repetition. He can gauge the actor's physical characteristics; his height and coloring, his bearing and deportment, a few glimmers of the true personality that occasionally peep through the professional persona he socially projects, but nothing very conclusive. He may learn more by calling him back two or three times, but even then, the actor's mask tends to solidify and the director's initial impressions are only reinforced. It is only in the rehearsal-situation that the actor gradually becomes known and, by that time if the director has miscalculated, it is too late. The painful business of compromise, relinquishing unattainable goals and settling for less, has already begun.

The actor's frustration in regard to the audition is that he or she knows that in the time allotted, it is impossible to show one's true mettle. The most that may be revealed is one's look, the timbre of one's voice and its ability to modulate varying states of emotion, but it says virtually nothing about the process by which raw material can be manufactured into first rate goods. That is, the actor is unable to reveal precisely what it is the director most wants to know: how will he or she respond to process?

CONDITION: Take your prepared speech, "To be or not to be" from Hamlet, and play it in the character of Macbeth contemplating the murder of Duncan. Saturate Hamlet's words with the character and attitudes of Macbeth and let the original text merely be a kind of sound-cover for the new character (Macbeth) in the altered situation (the contemplation of Duncan's murder).

Forcing the actor to dissociate his chosen character from one suddenly imposed by a director causes him to be in two places at the same time: textually in his monologue, but actually in a transplanted character and a different situation. It tells the director two things: a) how the actor copes with a 'direction' - how he fields an unanticipated new idea and b) how versatile he is at compartmentalizing his mind.

CONDITION: Take Romeo's text from the Balcony Scene and base it entirely on Richard III's courtship of Lady Anne. Romeo's words remain the same, but they are now colored and conditioned by the motives and character of Richard slyly trying to win the hand of the woman whose husband he has killed.

By conjuring up feelings which are at odds with the words the actor is speaking, he is obliged to draw on pure, non-verbal ingredients in order to express intention. In addition, he has to maintain the language of the original character whose scene has now been usurped - so he is obliged to juggle two balls without dropping either. Can he divide his mind in this way? Does he falter and stumble over his text? Does he make a bee-line for the 'Richard III cliche,' the twisted, humpbacked, music - hall sinister, or is there some semblance of this Richardized-Romeo which would make sense if he were actually tackling Gloucester in the other play? In seeking to answer these questions, the director obtains relevant information about the actor's capabilities.

CONDITION: Turn your speech of the Chorus from HENRY V into a) the spiel of a Hawker at an outdoor market selling cut-rate goods to eager housewives. Then into b) a Prosecuting Attorney demanding the death penalty from his jury. Then into c) a Commentator at a Fashion Show describing the fabric, cut and utility of the clothes being displayed by a succession of   fashion-models during on the runway. The speech thus played out in three different versions, switches from one to the other to the next, as I call out: "Hawker!" "Attorney!" or "Commentator!" - making sure that, in those lightning-changes, the original text transforms without a second's hesitation and that I see each different character clearly revealed. That done, go back to the Chrorus from HENRY V and perform it as originally conceived.

The speed with which an actor rings his changes, the definition of each changing character, the maintenance of the original text which no longer applies to the characters and situations delivering it, all of these things provide an insight into the actor's versatility and his ability to juggle antithetical ideas. If the actor balks at such an exercise, points out the illogicality of a hawker or an attorney mouthing Shakespeare's words from HENRY V, that too is informative about his mental outlook; his attitude to heterodoxy and experiment. Also, this exercise enables the director to learn something about his improvisational skills within the context of formal text - for at all times, the original text must be strictly observed - even as it is meaning things very different from what Shakespeare originally intended.

CONDITION: Take your soliloquy, Hamlet's "Oh that this too, too solid flesh would melt," and play it as it might be performed in the bombastic and high blown style of the 19th century - with as much vocal coloration and broadness of gesture as possible; in the finest tradition of the barnstorming ham-actors of the past. In short, as badly as you can.

The invitation to "tear a passion to tatters" is a very good gauge of precisely what size an actor is capable of achieving. Given the freedom to "act badly" often releases his tendency towards parody and comedy. If the actor has a sense of humor, it will be readily revealed in this exercise. If he has a full and vigorous vocal range, that too will become very apparent. If he manages to instill true passion into the overblown style which he's been encouraged to adopt, that is a good indication that, at some later juncture, and within the context of a true performance, he will be able to deliver the emotional goods. Lastly, it provides an inkling of just how kinetically free he may be, for indulging in gesture and broad movement, he immediately reveals his bodily freedom or lack of it when playing at full tilt.

CONDITION: Take your vigorous and energized version of "O, what a rogue and peasant slave am I" and play it as it might occur in a tight television close—up, played naturalistically, in a stream-of-consciousness and devoid of any bluster or bombast. That done, turn it into a comic monologue from a drawing-room comedy by Noel Coward wringing out of it every snide and sarcastic color possible. In the first instance, it is still Hamlet - albeit naturalized and reduced to the dimensions of television -screen; in the second, it is a dandified or dry character such as we often find in highly artificial comedies. A style very different from that appropriate to traditional Shakespeare in period dress.

If an actor can reduce the magnitude of rhetorical blank verse into the cadences of contemporary naturalism and still have it make sense, it indicates an aptitude for stylistic change which will come in handy no matter what plays are in the repertoire. The lower-keyed naturalistic truth of the TV close-up is precisely the living matter which has to be escalated when the classic is being played at full tilt. By watching it burn at a much lower intensity, it enables a director to analyze those lineaments-of-feeling which will eventually have to be increased. Playing frothy drawing-room comedy using rhetorical blank verse is yet another indication of the actor's versatility. If he can make it work with a soliloquy from Shakespeare, he can certainly make it work using Coward's own brittle language. The comic flair, the dryness, the show of superficiality - all of these things become even more conspicuous because of the incongruity of the text.

To reiterate: what the director most needs to know is how the actor 'works' - not how snugly he can wear the mask of an audition-piece which has become petrified through overuse. Since it is process he should be exploring, the audition must invite the actor to use the same interpretative muscles he will employ in grappling with a role. Is it a guarantee that mistakes will not be made? No. There is no such guarantee in the theatre, and the reason most directors like to use actors they already know is because it reduces the possibility of error and misconstruction. But even this can sometimes produce unsettling results - particularly when a director selects an actor for a type of role he has seen him perform admirably in the past - only to discover that something in the actor's nature resists duplicating the very quality for which he has been cast. The chemistry of each production is utterly unique, and the worst way to begin is with a load of preconceptions.

Acting often releases hidden potentialities and therefore, it is often the case that the actor whose personality seems furthest from the needs of a particular role can sometimes be the actor best suited to play it. What one should be casting is not the so-cial persona of the actor as established by past performances and perceived reputation, but the 'secret being' that inhabits that personality and is awaiting the opportunity to reveal itself to the world. To find *that*, one must remove the actor's mask, and to do that, one must recognize the disparity between how the actor sees himself, what he is, and what, under the stress of creative circumstances, he can become.

"Hedda"(adapted by Marowitz) Jenny Agutter (left) 1980 Round House Theatre

Donald Cooper Photography

*   *   *   *   *

IN THE BEGINNING

A First Reading is based on a number of deeply-entrenched beliefs.

    a) it enables the company to get some sense of the play in its
        entirety,

    b) it breaks the ice between performers and director,

    c) it provides an opportunity for the 'conception' of the play,
        both textually and scenically, to be outlined and dis
        cussed,

    d) it socializes, by means of an unpressured collective activity,
        all the persons who are going to undertake the work,

    e) one has to start somewhere, and a reading-of-the-play is as
        good a place as any.

Although all of these assumptions are sound, there are other aspects
to a First Reading that need to be considered.

There is often a desire on the part of certain actors to legitimize
their employment, to turn the reading into a demonstration of their talent. Sometimes actors reveal the reverse instinct firmly refusing to
'show their hand' - i.e. indicate the direction they intend to take. These
are the actors who are largely inaudible at the First Reading and make
a point of downplaying every moment as a clear signal that they are not
yet ready to commit to one choice or another. Then there are those
who, having already examined the script and begun to shape their performance, will render the text in a manner which, no matter how the

ensuing weeks may modify or refine it, is essentially the performance they will give on opening night.

There are those actors who cannot begin to take up the cudgels of their role until the intellectual implications of the piece have been thoroughly examined; who are eager to analyze the play's theme, the author's intentions, the director's assumptions, the designer's objectives, even the stage—manager's rules-of-procedure; who see their role as essentially a cog in a highly convoluted wheel.

As actors begin to verbalize their roles and insinuate the notions of their characters, other actors imperceptibly adapt to unexpected casting-choices and their colleague's quirky readings. The actor's anticipations, built up over days or weeks, sometimes months, collide with the reality of what they actually encounter around the table. The ignition has been switched on and, although no one is as yet sure of the route to be taken, the hum of the engine and the identity of the passengers - the front *and* backseat drivers - have already begun to make their presence felt.

Once the external characteristics of company members have been noted, the primary factor in a first reading is, of course, the text. The script, like a holy scroll, is clutched in everyone's hand and the sounds that emanate from the table are the author's words, often articulated for the very first time - an impression which persists even when the play is a revival or a classic. The clang of the First Reading always creates the impression of 'a first time;' the 'first time' this particular aggregate has that particular text in their mouths. In the beginning was the word.

In the 19th and well into the 20th century, it was often the custom for the author to read his play to the assembled cast. There was a certain obvious good sense about the practice. If a group of actors are intent on divining a playwright's meaning, hearing the work performed or recited in the accents of his own voice are about as clear an indication as one can possibly get, and since most playwrights are not usually actors, there is little danger of the playwright's line-readings being subsequently mimicked by the actors. There is alot to be said for the direct transference of intentionality from the author to the company. Even an author who is a wretched reader will be conveying meaning in a manner that may clarify the text for the actor. The other advantage is that the presence of the author's personality brings with it a certain ring of authenticity which, in the imagination of talented actors, can be assimilated and utilized. When G. Bernard Shaw read his play to his assembled actors, the radiance of the Shavian intellect must have insinuated subtleties and nuances which no director could as effectively translated into stage-directions. But as the director gained prominence, the playwright tended to recede into the background and the first reading became the exclusive province of the interpreters.

But long before the actors arrive on the scene, the author, director and the designers have anticipated what they are going to do. The director in particular, has roughed out a 'direction' for himself - even if it's based only on a hunch, an unarticulated impulse, a vague inclination. If he has really done his homework, he has a fairly clear inkling of what he is after and some idea about the size of the obstacles he is going to encounter. If there *is* an author to consult, he has an even clearer idea of the production's architecture and where the foundations have to be laid.

By starting with the 'word,' there is a tacit assumption that the object of everyone's labor is language and that the mission of rehearsals is the assembly and refinement of that language into some sort of final construct. The 'performance' to come is a performance of language.

But as rehearsals progress, it soon becomes apparent that words are only the tiles of the building being assembled; that without an inner structure, there is no roof on to which to place the tiles. A shifting emotional and intellectual substructure has to be built virtually from the ground up.

When Joan Littlewood began rehearsals for her production of Brendan Behan's "The Hostage," the whole of the first day was spent with the actors marching in a strict, military fashion on the roof of the building. This was not directorial sadism but a clear understanding that in order to prepare the play, the actors had to experience the kind of regimentation that prevailed in a British prison. Similarly, when we began work on John Herbert's "Fortune and Men's Eyes" at The Open Space Theatre, the actors were treated to a rigorous regime of yard-exercises which was standard drill in Canadian reformatories. On the first day of rehearsals of "Hedda Gabler" in Bergen, Norway, the members of the company were asked to improvise their testimony at a judicial hearing where the shooting of Eilert Loevborg was being investigated by a police tribunal. The actors, all operating in character, were obliged to answer questions about themselves, about Hedda, the shooting incident and anything else put by their questioners. What little background they had on their characters was urgently expanded under the stress of the questioning which sought to unearth relevant information both about themselves and their relationship to the victim. The rehearsal was spent trying to create the psychological fabric of the small Norwegian town in which these characters lived so that when they retired to their respective niches, they had some idea of the society they inhabited. Also, it demonstrated how characters who led essentially private lives might react to a public situation; information which could then be fed back into the play.

Before the sculptor begins sculpting, he selects the stone, clay, bronze, wood or other material on which he is going to work. The painter also makes certain preliminary decisions: oils, water-colors, charcoal, crayon, etc. The actor's first task is to create the psychic world his character will eventually inhabit. This has virtually nothing to do with language. It is the ambiance and atmosphere out of which words will eventually spring, but its roots are not verbal. *What* they are will differ from play to play, but if one is going to start properly, the first decision, and unquestionably the hardest, is to try to evoke the social ambiance and psychological climate in which the play is going to unfold.

The society in "Measure For Measure" is tumultuous, rebellious. The Duke is leaving because the city is up in arms. The severity of its laws has created profound unrest. There is a palpable sense of growing disorder, even revolt. If this is thought to be the background from which the Duke flees setting Angelo in his place, it is essential to conjure up the feel of such a society before Angelo steps on stage, and before the Duke makes his departure. The creation of that social disarray will condition everything that follows: Angelo's relationship with Escalus, with the Provost, with a novice seeking a reprieve for her brother's life, etc. If, on the other hand, a director decides that the social disorder in Vienna is not the determining factor; that, for instance, the corruption of the state is so deeply embedded and its authorities so firmly in control that revolt is unthinkable, then a different set of priorities come into play. Then perhaps, one has to create that tense, bureaucratic atmosphere that one associates with Poland or Czechoslovakia during the Soviet occupation. Without first establishing the parameters of the given society, the situations and incidents take place merely on a stage. A stage not imbued with the social and psychological atmospheres of the people that inhabit it, can never transform into the imaginative world of the play.

If, in the beginning, one relinquishes the script and through improvisation and experiment, begins to explore the vital issues contained in the play, the actor's mind is set free. He does not yet have a grasp of character and his crutch, the script, is knocked out from under him. There is a danger that by discarding his literary frame of reference (the script), he may wander into areas which are irrelevant and even contradictory to the play's purposes. But there is a value even in these diversions, for once he begins to compare his instinctive with his considered choices, he has a clearer picture of what does or does not work in the given context. The surest way of uprooting erroneous choices is to be sharply brought up by the error of one's ways. When this happens, the 'correction' is not administered from without by a director, but by the actor himself who, having personally experienced something that 'doesn't work' can now hone into something that does. But the greater advantage of exploring wider territory through improvisation and exercise is that the onus for discovery is placed firmly onto the actor. He is not experimenting only with the writer's materials - debating inflections and arranging rhythms - but using his own sensibility to explore those issues and ideas posited by the playwright. It confers a sense of personal power to the actor which is independent of both playwright and director. When these exploits are over, what he brings back to the rehearsals is something that could never have been found if he had remained tethered to the script and locked in its language.

The rationale for all such experimentation is the enrichment of the play and the intentions of the production. In an ideal situation, it is the director and playwright who are encouraging the actor into this zone of free-trade in the hope that their own aims will be more fully realized. It is a paradox of play-production that the more unshackled the actor is from the text and the mise-en-scene, the richer both become. The reverse situation (which obtains in most theatres of the world) where the director helps the actor into a straitjacket and the playwright inserts a tape of his dialogue into his brain, is almost always destructive to all three parties. In nine cases out of ten, the actor's inestimable potential is never realized because it is never tapped.

Unless one is working with an ensemble or a permanent company, the director's first requisite is to create a collectivity out of the disparate people that make up his cast. A reading sometimes only increases the isolation that already exists. Actors sheltering behind the fortress of their scripts dig even deeper into their enclaves making only a kind of aural contact with each other. Whereas, if the first thing a company does is discover each other kinetically, sharing their energy and conveying their personal rhythms to one another, the collective spirit in its raw state is immediately encountered.

In many ad hoc productions I've begun with the Work-Out detailed in the Exercises chapter of this book. These are free-styled, kinetic exercises using sound and movements as a way of tapping something more basic in the actor than his or her ability to read lines and insinuate feelings. It is a radical way of saying hello. A little like being invited into a strange house where a drunken party is in full swing. If one can enter into the spirit of that party, the Work Out tends to bulldoze inhibitions and peak personal creativity. Sometimes it makes actors feel foolish because at base, the Work Out is a kind of childsplay. But if the director acknowledges the foolishness beforehand and explains that it simply doesn't matter how silly one actually looks or feels, it can often provoke the freedom and anarchy which informed our respective childhoods. The imaginative flow that stems from that atmosphere creates the fiber out of which the very best rehearsals are fashioned.

The more guarded and conservative actors will detest it; the actors already confident of their powers will view it as a waste of time. Some actors will feel it is a reversion to the games and exercises they associate with drama school and construe it as an insult to their professionalism. I have had actors walk out of the Work-Out and resign their roles. I have had others burst into tears and drown in confusion. Since rehearsal time is always precious and the tyrannical clock is always ticking, why spend hours playing games and employing sounds-and-movements that have no apparent relevance to the task at hand? These are all sensible questions and I have often asked them of myself, but I have found that the hours devoted to such Work-Outs have developed the mesh out of which an ensemble is held together. When, for one reason or another, I have discarded the practice, the company was not as whole, the collective intelligence not as sharp, the interplay not as sensitive.

I can easily visualize a production approach which creates the very same ensemble togetherness by adhering to the most conventional practices; a reading, a plotting-out-of-moves, a selection of tempi, pauses and other kinds of dramatic punctuation, a slate of previews and an opening. In London, I have often seen ad hoc companies of actors eschewing any such preliminaries produce startling collective results.

But almost always those actors came from a shared background, the same or similar kinds of drama academies, seasons in rep, supporting or leading roles in West End productions; techniques honed by one night stands in arduous touring situations. Although never consciously acknowledged, these actors actually sprang from the same cultural milieu, were forged in the same crucible and, as a result, spoke the same language, developed the same facilities and, by and large, shared the same artistic values. Their 'ensemble' may not have been as clearly defined as the Old Vic or the Comedie Francaise, but the same principles of artistic coalition governed their work and unified their character.

The Work-Out is a compression of the same kind of variegated experience aimed at creating the interconnecting vertebrae that develop among actors who have had the advantage of playing with one another over a long period of time and under various conditions. It is a calculated means of reaching the deeper tissue of actors which, in many production situations, is barely ever touched. It is like swimming in the ocean rather than a lap-pool; an attempt to feel the full swirl of everything that constitutes the actor's inner being so that when the panoply of the play is put into place, there will be more going on behind its walls.

In a verbally dominated theatre such as obtains in London or Paris, it is very easy for rehearsals to begin and end with acrobatic verbiage. The play becomes the acoustical expression of its author's language without those deeper recesses which theoretically bring that language to life. Actors, writers and directors spend most of their hours talking. Audiences arrive expecting to tune in language. Critics often tend to assess what they have heard rather than what they have seen. The language-trap is as deadly in the theatre as it is in society. In both places, we are constantly searching for ways to transcend it or give it interior significance. Beginning with actions, tapping into our lexicon of sounds and exploring movements are ways of avoiding the danger that a production will be nothing more than a linguistic facade. It is not an alternative to pithy and plangent language (and certainly not in the case of 17th and 18th century classics which are essentially language-constructs), but it is another way to root out the treasures of a great or good play and, when conscientiously applied, provides a framework in which words and actions truly coalesce.

*   *   *   *   *

BEYOND MISE-EN-SCENE

As soon as rehearsals begin, the engendering minds of both performer and director become activated. Something in the text, an idea
triggered by an acting-partner, a personal recollection or a director's
casual remark, invites the actor towards a particular proposition and he
proceeds to test it. Soon he is on the scent of a discovery; an insight, a
twist, a conditioning truth. The role acts upon him like a magic elixir.
Every swallow adds new flavor to his conception; every emphasis and
inflection suggests a new angle, a preference, a possibility. The actor's
mind, translated into vocal and physical impulses, gradually spins the
wheel that weaves the characterization.

The director, in close proximity to his actor, follows along the same
path. He is on hand to share the actor's hunches, his discoveries, his
wrong-turnings. But he too is weaving a tapestry and its pattern is much
wider than the actor's since he is taking threads from the playwright and
the designers as well. Where the actor is assiduously looking through
a microscope, the director is mapping out an aerial photograph.

The actor sometimes ranges into areas which are beyond bounds -
which draws the focus away from the immediacy of the play and the
gravitational pull of its stated purpose. The director is just as liable as
the actor to be led astray. His olfactory sense is also tempted by allur-
ing aromas. He too is prone to take circuitous routes, to get tangled in
the underbrush, to lose his way. It is not so much the blind leading the

blind as fellow-travelers walking through a dark wood and sharing a single flashlight. Now one leads and the other follows; then the reverse.

It has been said that casting represents ninety percent of any production, and it is true that as soon as a particular actor is chosen, his traits, his temperament, his personal qualities specifically color the outlines set down by the playwright. A veteran director asked by an actress who her character actually was, replied: "You!" Once a performer has been cast, that is an inescapable truth. Every character, no matter how originally conceived, takes on the mental and physical coloration of the performer. This is so obvious it is easy to forget it; to be misled into thinking that the actor, instead of revealing his nakedness in the role is actually concealing himself in its disguises. But intrinsically, acting is about revelation and not concealment and a man puts on a mask not to hide himself, but to express himself more forcefully to others.

If the selection of the actor constitutes the lion's share of the interpretation because an actor's physical and psychological constituents determine every outcome, what is the director's task? Surely, not only to organize the traffic of the stage, for no great creative resources are needed to accomplish that. The director is not merely there to objectify the actor's performance, to tell him when he is standing in a good or bad light, when he is audible or inaudible.

Essentially, the director is there to heal and temper. To heal the sickness which is inflicted by actors upon themselves and to temper the fire of their emotional heat. "Healing the actor's sickness" is not a fanciful phrase, for in every worthwhile production, the actor infects himself with a number of toxins derived from his fictional situation and stimulates himself by powerful memories from his own experience.

One cannot play Richard III or Iago, Shylock or Tamburlaine without stirring the juices of one's own malice and hatred. A Richard not nourished by an actor's most murderous instincts, misses the mark; a Shylock not stirred by prejudice and driven by avarice cannot help dilute the acetic mixture which swirls in that character's bloodstream. To awaken these qualities is to stir in the actor's metabolism some of the strongest and most dangerous emotions that reside in human beings; the compulsion towards jealousy, the obsession to dominate, the desire to destroy. Like an exorcist, the director accompanies the actor down the gullies of his worst nature, prodding his most malevolent forces but, at the same time, monitoring them so that they do not overwhelm the actor nor incapacitate his performance. The healing consists of filtering those toxins into the vessels of the role, so that it is a sound, and not an unsound, person who confronts the public. 'Tempering,' in its painterly connotation, involves diluting colors in order to bring them into a proper balance - just as in its metallurgical sense, it means softening the scorching temperatures of steel or iron and reheating them at a lower temperature to make them malleable. The actor relies on the director to accomplish these feats, and because powerful factors are involved, it is delicate work.

The director then, in order to 'heal' and 'temper,' must first engender sickness and heat; must draw the actor down to his lowest depths where his most primitive feelings dwell so that the most powerful ingredients are being tossed into that crucible which will ultimately produce the performance. That is, if you like, his most quintessential task; his most arduous and most seminal, but of course, he has lesser functions which are just as necessary. He is not exclusively a magus or a medium, he is also a docent and an interlocutor, an anecdotalist and a coach.

Because an idea tossed into a fertile mind can effloriate an actor's imagination, the director must constantly dispense graphic imagery, pose challenging questions and offer provocative conceits. This almost goes without saying. Tossing off a fecund idea can do for a susceptible actor what an exhilarating quotation from the gospel can for a religious zealot. Because the director has the power to 'inspire' actors, he should use it cunningly and sparingly. Because his words tempt actors to leap onto fast-moving freight-trains, he must be mindful of their ultimate destinations. In troubled productions, the stickiest problems are often the result of an ambiguous or half-baked idea casually tossed out by a loose-lipped director. The germ of an unthought-out idea can be responsible for an ineradicable fallacy from which there may be no turning back.

Useful as verbal stimuli may be, they do not begin to compare with vested experience - that is, a sensation or an insight which an actor obtains as a result of performing an action, extending a moment, or reversing a choice.

By 'performing an action,' I mean placing a speech or a scene in a physical context radically removed from the one indicated by the script. (i.e. Hamlet's soliloquy "Oh that this too too solid flesh would melt" performed on the floor in the embryo position, crouched inside a broom-closet, locked inside a trunk.). In order to simulate the psychic state out of which a dramatic moment emanates, it is sometimes useful to physically duplicate that state. A scene in which a character is buoyant and carefree might be rehearsed with the actor skipping down the aisle or soaring on a swing. A speech in which a character feels threatened may be played by the actor moving stealthily through the theatre, probing each nook and cranny while delivering his text. An actress try-ing to seduce a character with her feminine wiles may deliver the speech while performing a striptease or flagrantly pressing her body up against her partner. In every case, the physicalization of the scene externalizes what the scene is intrinsically about. It puts actors into a different, usu-ally more exaggerated, relationship to the material and has the advan-tage of freeing them from blocking which they may not yet be able to justify emotionally. The relocation into the exercise-state is itself liber-ating as it breaks the rigid pattern of conventional staging, and usually, anything useful found in the exercise-situation can be retained when the original mise-en-scene is reinstated.

In most rehearsal situations, actors test readings and inflections - seek new colors or rhythms. But if actors, using radical vocal and phys-ical probes, were to explore different inner-states, they might uncover character-shifts which would automatically affect the reading of their lines. Our language takes on different texture and coloration depend-ing on what is going on in the deepest reaches of our psyche. We mut-ter or hesitate, shout or scream, are direct or tangential depending on the interplay of forces swirling about in our nature. Unlike actors, we do not 'choose' to emphasize a certain word or hover in the interstices of a pause; sounds and rhythms arise in us because of the way we are ex-pressing, suppressing or camouflaging our feelings. But the actor, working from the outside in, experiments with vocal dynamics in order to gauge their emotional effect both on himself and, by inference, on his audience. It is largely an intellectual process and involves the con-scious placement of signs and signals on the author's text; a kind of semiotic notation applied by the actor.

Through the use of Extensions, the actor, assiduously looking for the exact quantity of feeling necessary to achieve a particular effect, experiences that effect whole-hog - far in excess of what is required. Hamlet baiting and then castigating Ophelia in the Nunnery Scene fully unleashes his contempt on the girl he ostensibly once loved and who has now been coerced into a conspiracy against him. His wild fury and her terrified response to it overflow the scene. He is maniacal, and uncontrollable; she, confused and petrified. Both, having played in excess of the requisite feelings can now begin to reduce the temperature of the scene. Having experienced the height of the emotions the scene was capable of, the actors have a clearer idea as to which point to pull back to. But wherever that point may be, it will now be conditioned by what the scene felt like in full flood. The Extension, by giving the scene a topmost point, more clearly suggests its appropriate level. But the information has been arrived at through emotional experience rather than intellectual analysis.

Reversals have the advantage of informing the actor of roads not taken and choices rejected. An actor playing a virtuous character (Henry V let's say) by feeding his speeches through the persona of an evil character, (the Duke of Gloucester, let's say) pulls the moral meridian into a completely different direction. Contradictory as it may seem, there are still moments in which even the most virtuous character is capable of malice or vindictiveness (in the Case of Henry V, when suddenly turning on the traitors Scroop, Cambridge and Grey), and the most villainous seized by contrition (Richard III responding to the ghostly visitation of the victims he has killed.) We all insist to each other, according to the Stanislavsky doctrine, that we should try to find the opposite moral traits in the characters we play; that we should look for the good in bad characters and vice verse. By *experiencing* reverse-actions, we not only assume morally opposite traits, but character-qualities only barely hinted at in our roles. For example: the budding sexuality of Juliet; the wantonness of Desdemona; the suppressed carnality of Isabella; the fanaticism behind Shylock's religious orthodoxy, etc. No character can ever be a monolith representing only one overriding characteristic. All characters are compounded of traits which often are contradictory, paradoxical, and contrary to expectation. The more colors we have in our palates and the more we mix them into our design, the richer our final result.

The conventional way is, having decoded our super-objective and the objectives and actions which constitute the role, to pile up the building-blocks into one vertical structure. 'The other way' is to create a series of pathways into the character and follow them wherever they may lead - no matter how contradictory or perverse their destinations on the assumption that the final product, having more facets to choose from, will create a character more varied and less predictable.

All of this happens or does not happen, depending on the delicate, often ambivalent, relationship built up between actor and director. Essentially, the actor has the choice of two pacts with the director; the Napoleonic or the Faustian. Under the terms of the first, the director receives the diligent efforts of his rank-and-file and strategically utilizes them for maximal effect. Under the terms of the Faustian pact, he promises to provide visions, spectacles and magic so long as the actor will cede him his soul. Needless to say, most actors would rather be mustered into service and be told what to do rather than risk their lives for a dubious immortality.

*   *   *   *

When the production has reached the run-through stage, and before the technical complement is added, the time is ripe to test the sub-text. This can be done in three ways: through sounds, movement and music.

1) The actors, abandoning the text per se but retaining the rhythm of their lines, are asked to create sounds in place of the play's prescribed language. The sounds convey the underlying intention behind the text. By retaining the rhythms of their speeches, each actor will know precisely where they are in the script, but by abandoning the text per se, the actors are put into direct contact with their underlying emotions. The sounds must not be arbitrary. They should convey the 'character' of what is going on at any given moment in the play. (i.e. sibilant whispers for conspiratorial moments, accented grunts for growing hostility, moans and cries for moments of pain or anguish, etc). The actors do not premeditate these sounds; they are improvised according to the impulses which already exist beneath the text. Once the scene has been performed in sounds with the rhythms of the speeches retained, it can be repeated with the rhythms forsaken and more generalized sounds used to convey the content of each beat. This will produce a tighter and more compressed version of the former exercise and should only be attempted after the rhythmic sounds have been played out.

2) A less radical version of this exercise is for the actors to adopt a variety of accents and dialects which have some affinity with the roles they are playing, (i.e. a German accent for a rough, brutal character, a French accent for a dominantly lyrical character, a Japanese accent for a mannered and socially-armored character, a Brooklyn accent for a crude, unmannerly type, etc etc). In all such 'runs,' in order to avoid the exercise becoming mechanical, it is useful to shuttle between sounds, accents and straightforward performance of the scenes as rehearsed, the director cueing these shifts at will.

3) At a more advanced stage, the actors are asked to treat the play as if it were a ballet, abandoning the text and translating the sub-text entirely into dance movements. Although this exercise is often referred to as 'ballet,' there is no limitation as to the styles of dance which may be included: modern, jazz, ethnic, modern, free-style, tap-dance etc. The 'balletic' choices are conditioned by the nature of the scene and the actions of its characters. Again, nothing is premeditated. The actors spontaneously select these movements as the scene progresses, (It is essential in all these exercises that a highly efficient stage-manager sticks close to the script so that dropped lines (which are frequent in such exercise-situations) can be cued as soon as required.)

4) The play is now conceived entirely as an opera, the text as the opera's libretto, and all the textual material is sung by the actors. The music's originality is irrelevant. This is not an exercise to see who can improvise ravishing melodies. The actors are encouraged to find musical expressions which correspond to the feelings embedded in their text. Since the text is now being sung, it will necessarily become elongated and every speech will run longer. (Almost always, the language becomes more precise} Here too, there is no restriction as to the style of the music. One character may feel 'grand opera' is appropriate for his character; another something more modern or 'pop;' a third may opt for jazz or rock 'n roll. There need be no stylistic uniformity in the music and the 'music' itself need be whatever kind of melodic expression the actor feels appropriate to his character and scene.

5) Once the company has developed these various exercise-idioms, they should be encouraged to mix them so that, for instance, one character is singing the text while another dances it; a third will be using

sounds exclusively while a fourth will be playing in accents. A fifth may simply be whispering his or her role while a sixth plays it in the conventional manner, as rehearsed. It may be best for the director to assign the idiom for each actor rather than to leave it to the actors themselves so that the idiomatic choices best suited to each character can be consciously selected.

When this kind of 'testing of the sub-text' is first begun, there is inevitably a kind of absurdity in the air. Actors who have been used to diligently building their moments with brick and mortar are suddenly asked to play with their choices as if they were children frolicking in a sandbox. Moments of true pathos and intense feeling turn into ridiculous parodies of what has been assiduously prepared over a period of many weeks. Directors should be prepared for the exercises to pass through this phase of absurdity before any benefits accrue. After a while, the weirdness of what is being attempted wears off and the creative task of transforming sub-text into other artistic forms is taken for the great challenge it is. Obviously, these kinds of tactics work best in companies where actors have a shared language and a built-in artistic togetherness, but it can also be beneficial in ad hoc companies where a conducive atmosphere exists.

These exercises restore a sense of child's play to what is often serious and formidable work. These put the actor directly in touch with currents of feeling and thought which sometimes grow stale and can even atrophy after many weeks of slogging rehearsal. If the grasp of a scene's sub-text is solid and secure, there is no reason in the world why it cannot be sung or danced, expressed in sounds and gestures. One is simply reconstituting in a different form what one has already created. The abandonment of text can often be quite liberating. The actor sees, with a clarity which conventional rehearsal never allows, precisely what he has constructed and therefore, can test it in a way that is not possible when enveloped in the playwright's text.

Of course, the reason for testing the sub-text and exercising the musculature of a production is to enhance and better define the performance-proper. When the actors return to the play after their bizarre journey into music and dance, sound and parody, there is often a new ease and relaxation in their interaction. The return to text and mise-en-scene is a kind of celebration of the production's original sanity. Often, discoveries are made during the exercises which alter or embellish what actors and directors have previously set. This 'testing of the sub-text'z validates or puts into question the choices which make up the production - and the best time to do that is just before the hatches are battened down and the tyranny of technical rehearsals banishes all opportunity to experiment.

These actions and activities are not only the constituents of an acting-approach but the attitudes and values of a philosophy. The philosophy behind Stanislavsky's system was rooted in a reverence for scientific rationalism which people such as Zola, Pasteur, Spencer and Darwin had fostered in the 19th century. An attitude to life which believed that man, being primarily a social animal, could be analyzed and defined according to certain fixed criteria. When Freud entered the picture, it widened to include the unconscious mind but essentially, it was a continuation of the idea that man was reducible to atoms and molecules, instincts and drives. In that kind of mental climate, it made perfect sense to say that a character has an 'objective,' that he overcomes obstacles and employs tactics to achieve it; that a play had a 'premise' and its constituent parts represented the proposition by which that premise was demonstrated. Everything was bounded by a provable logic that was unassailable, mainly because most people believed it. I say 'most people' for there were always those like Jarry, Meyerhold, Artaud and Vitrac who even then questioned the validity of that mechanistic universe; who believed that the unseen was as potent as what could be seen and in many ways, more potent for being invisible.

The acting-theory which emanated from that world-view is still the one that dominates the theatre and is largely subscribed to by the majority of those people practicing the art-form. But the changes in sensibility have been sweeping. A telephone is a simulacrum of the 19th century. You pick up the receiver, you dial, you connect with the other party, you convey a message. A computer is a simulacrum of the latter part of the 20th century. An open sesame to the Information Highway, it combines innumerable intersecting points; it glories in its complexity and disdains roads with one-way traffic. It is intrinsically interactive. It requires constant 'upgrading' because there is no end to the ingenuity with which it harnesses intelligence and extends the borders of communication. Human beings are neither telephones nor computers, but where computer technology and acting-theory coalesce is in their notions of pluralism and complexity.

The theatre became modern the moment it realized that things were not one way, but one way and another. You might say it was Chekhov who first instituted meaningful ambiguity, the stock-in-trade of writers such as Becket, Ionesco, Pinter and Stoppard - but you can find just as much 'meaningful ambiguity' in Shakespeare, so it's hard to ascribe it specifically to the end of the 19th century. But whatever its historical roots, it has become the artistic fashion of the times. We snicker at the moral polarity of melodrama, decry it as 'bombastic and unreal,' use it as a stick to beat our theatrical predecessors. Pat answers, we now believe, cannot be true ones. The more levels we can ascertain, the more contradictions we discover, the more persuaded we are that things are 'true to life.'

And yet in acting, we pursue a methodology that is almost the reverse of these beliefs. One that codifies our sense of human nature instead of acknowledging the fact that it is unclassifiable. In the theatre as in life, what strikes us most powerfully is the incongruous action, the uncharacteristic move, the sudden lurch away from consistency, and yet when we undertake to simulate reality, we do it in such a way as to remove the incongruous and stay doggedly 'in character.'

A computer is not a more elaborate version of the abacus, just as a television-set is not simply a 'telephone' with pictures. There are congeries of new ideas and technologies behind each of those instruments and they have ushered us into, not only a new kind of life but, a new way of experiencing life. An acting-theory that is worth its salt must spring from and relate back to the intellectual currents of contemporary life. Otherwise, it falsifies the depiction of that life by perpetuating ideas from a former time.

But new ideas are merely variations and extensions of former ideas (although occasionally, entirely new concepts arrive which thoroughly wipe the slate clean) and so the actor has constantly to modify and appropriate, adapt and revise, correlate the dynamics of his craft with the esthetic for which it is being employed. The greatest danger is for him to assume that no matter what external changes are taking place, fundamentals remain the same. It is a disturbing truth, but an inescapable one, that art, like politics, is capable of full-scale reversals, total transformations and revolutions which wholly destroy old orders and replace them with new ones.

THE STITCH OF THOUGHT

"Actually the word drama is a transliteration of
the Greek *opautu*, which means a thing done, while
theatre is a transliteration of the Greek *oeatpov*, which
means a seeing place. Even the word audience, meaning
those who listen, is derived from the Latin and therefore represents a later idea of playgoing. It is from the
use of two Greek words and one Latin word that a most
useful hint is given us as to the very first dramatic
values."

> Carelton, in 'Light Up
> The Sky' by Moss Hart

In its origins, theatre was 'a seeing place.' A hearth, a clearing, a place between large rocks. With the advent of classical drama, it became a seeing-*and*-a-hearing place and the concept of a 'stage' was born. It has become many things since but essentially, it has directed itself to the senses of sight and sound and so it is understandable that over the last few centuries, theatre-training has traditionally separated the voice from the body, the sight from the sound. While certain cultures have produced actors who can speak and others who can move and occasionally actors who can do both, the false dichotomy between voice and body remains.

Most theatre-schools assume that the separation is temporary, and that having trained the actors' voices and then given them 'movement,' both disciplines automatically coalesce in the act of performance, but there are too many instances where voice and movement have not blended into the actor's being; too many instances where impressive effects in vocalism or kinetics have not been organically assimilated into the actor's performance. Indeed, there have been instances where the development of the actor's voice has disfigured his ability to create natural performances and instances, particularly in England, where performers have become 'acting voices' disconnected from the physical musculature that produces fully integrated interpretations. John Gielgud, according to critic Kenneth Tynan, was England's greatest actor "from the neck up" - which is a backhanded way of saying he was not an actor at all but a beautifully-modulated speaking-machine which stroked the auditory sensors. By the same token, we have all come across actors who appear to be almost physically handicapped by their bodies; who are resonant and syrupy but whom we find it hard to look at because they lack ease and natural flow.

In England and less so in America, speech-training has become interlarded with notions of class and social status. In England, accent is an unmistakable sign of social position and the class-divisions - working, middle, upper-middle and upper - all have their recognizable tones of voice. In the late 50s and 60s, when these social stratifications began to break down in the English theatre and actors with regional accents found themselves more and more on West End stages, this was seen by many as an encroachment upon 'good standards of speech,' which was a euphemism for uppityness - members of the working-classes infiltrating areas from which they had previously been barred. What made actors like Albert Finney, Peter O'Toole and Nicol Williamson remarkable, talent notwithstanding, was the fact that they spoke in accents very different from those of John Gielgud, Laurence Olivier and Ralph Richardson and represented a social class which was thought to be at odds with what was highest in dramatic art. In schools like the

Royal Academy of Dramatic Art and the Central School of Speech & Drama, rigorous efforts were made to 'anglicize' the accents of talented working-class actors with rough, regional accents and, by the time they graduated, this usually resulted in a uniformity of diction which consoled the members of the old order and ironically, comforted the actors themselves many of whom equated standard BBC-English with an escalation of both social and professional status. By the mid 60s, all of this had changed - and today there are English actors who glory in their regional accents - although they are quick to point out that they can speak as 'posh' as anyone from Oxford or Cambridge, should the occasion arise.

Speech is not a given; it is a floating influence; extended exposure to one particular kind of diction often affects our own. A protracted period in England gradually transformed my New York nasality into something resembling middle-class British speech - although it was never accepted as such in England - just as in my own country, Americans tended to recoil from my 'phony British accent' which was nothing more than hard, consonantal speech with soft rather than flattened vowel-sounds. Once back in America, the residue of English diction began to fall away and eventually, my somewhat succinct American speech was taken to be New England and, as such, culturally acceptable.

Speech-training is a useful way of affecting a superficial personality transformation, (i.e. in 'Pygmalion'). It is a cultural ruse teeming with social, even political, connotations. It is the dough out of which all accents and dialects are baked. But it must be distinguished from voice-training which is direct contact with the physiological apparatus which give actors resonance, precision, texture and projection. Most acting tuition concerns itself with what it pretentiously calls 'the instrument,' implying that once fully developed, the actor can play some pretty hot licks on his well-developed voice-box. In recent years, it has been thought of as an open sesame to effective classical acting and there are innumerable misguided speech and voice specialists who sincerely believe that speaking clearly is a primary factor in acting Shakespeare correctly. For about a hundred years, the technical aspects of voice-production were ostentatiously dissociated from acting and, in the past ten or twenty years, efforts have been made to restore them. Although not as rigid as it was, the old dichotomy still exists.

*   *   *   *   *   *

What is often overlooked in speech and voice training is that, under the stress of certain emotions, the voice necessarily becomes a strained and constricted instrument which goes right against all the high precepts inculcated by the voice-teacher. The sound an actor makes is not a specimen of pharyngeal or thoraxial coordination but an utterance conditioned by psychological and emotional conditions. A good speaking voice becomes a travesty when a character such as Hamlet or Macbeth is in his final death-throes since anyone in such a physical condition cannot possibly speak well. That is an extreme example, but by the same token, the timbre of a character's voice pretending to something he is not, concealing a rage or suffering an extreme social embarrassment, has to take on a color appropriate to the emotions being expressed. Every moment of every role imposes certain qualities of pitch and volume, color and texture which render the sound of those feelings plausible.

But speech training tends to concentrate exclusively on the apparatus that produces language rather than the combination of elements that produce acting. Certainly there are large stretches in plays, classical and modern, where there is a necessity for language to be clear, crisp and concise; where diction rather than feeling is paramount. But are there any moments in any play when a character under the stress of some action or another, some sub-textual pressure, does not imbue speech with dramatic color of some kind? No play is the equivalent of a speech-exercise and no role can ever be defined exclusively in terms of its vocal components. To be a character, whatever the context, is to speak with dramatic purpose and to convey emotional, rather than purely linguistic, information.

The speech-teacher and the vocal-coach take the actor's vocal equipment lubricate it, strengthen and develop it, teach it fluency and variety, resonance and precision then hand it to the director who, in the course of developing character and engendering conflict, tends to discard all the actor has previously been told. For in expressing emotion or reacting to stress, the actor cannot possibly have speech-technique in the forefront of his mind. By then, the instrument is already operative or it isn't, but to make the actor aware of acoustical considerations when he is theoretically being blown about in the 'whirlwind of his passion' is to intrude a technical consciousness where it clearly does not belong. The piano-tuner's job is done with when the concert recitalist sits down to play and the voice-teacher should not intrude pointers on breathing and vocal-color when the actor is engrossed in his role.

In recent years, to overcome the dichotomy between vocal and acting interpretation, voice-production has figured more and more prominently in production per se. It is common, particularly in classical works, to see voice-teachers credited along with directors and designers, the general assumption being that whereas directors have the responsibility for the actor's interpretation, 'specialists' are also on hand to make sure their language is correct and efficacious. I have known cases where voice-teachers have been 'assigne' to rehearsals to insure that the actor's 'instrument' is working at peak efficiency, but I have never known such external assistance to have anything but an intrusive effect. It is an irritating incursion and stems from the fact that we are living in a world where the 'specialist' has horned his or her way into areas where, not only do they not belong but where they subvert other 'specialists' assigned to far more taxing work.

An actor who has not already learned the metre of blank verse and the secrets of scansion, the knowledge of where to take breaths and how to project forward speech has no business being on the stage in the first place. It is as silly to think that his inadequacies can be rectified during rehearsals as it is to believe that a number of helpful hints shouted out from the wings can assist a singer who has not yet learned to sight-read. But of course, every actor's voice needs regular lubrication before a performance in order to operate at peak efficiency, but that vocal limbering should not be separated from the body's tune-up, but be a part of it. The curious phenomenon in most theatres before the curtain goes up is the actor exercising his vocal cords either sitting before his dressing-room mirror or standing in the Green Room as if the rest of the bodily apparatus would automatically come alive once the voice had been energized.

Voice has always been thought of as the vessel for speech or song. In other words, the handmaiden of language or music. And yet since Artaud and latterly Grotowski, it is clear that the theatre can also be a place where pure sound can convey dramatic information unfettered by grammar or syntax, logic or sense. When we think of cries or groans, shrieks or wails, we always think of them as emotional punctuations in naturalistic situations.   When words fail and emotion is too overwhelming, we accept that people may give voice to feelings that cannot be contained in words.

Artaud was constantly searching for a 'new language' which would transcend the logical-positivism of comprehensible speech.   He assumed that gesture and movement could be used as auxiliaries to this 'new language,' but realistically speaking, if you employ only gesture and movement, you fall into mime and if you abdicate language, you are also abdicating civilization and sinking back into the quagmire of primitivism from which, happily, we have raised ourselves.   But as a tool to discover the greater significance of the sounds we make to one another when we converse, there is alot to be said for tracing our feelings downward from language and back to their sonic roots.   Although we assume that language articulates our feelings, we often forget that it is never through language alone.   The color, timbre, intensity and character of the sound that clings to speech is what conveys its emotional character, and that emanates not from the cervical cortex or the diaphragm, but from some precognitive zone whose ancestry is older than civilization.   Once we accept that psychology is only the threshold of consciousness, we are led to the conclusion that our wrath, our hunger, our fear and all our most powerful drives are derivations of the same emotions that stirred Cro-Magnon Man.   Just as conventional theatre-training stops at the discovery of sub-text, so does our voice-training content itself with the physiological requirements that maintain speech.   If it didn't, if it went beyond the known chemistry of voice-production, it would more usefully connect up with the actor's needs.

*   *   *   *   *

Kristin Linklater is one of the most sensible voice-teachers in the country, but even she has posited a theory which begs the whole question of voice training. "The problems," she writes in *Freeing The Natural Voice* "all stem from the separation of the voice from the person, and their root causes can be found in psycho-physical conditioning by family, education and environment."

If that is the case, the actor needs the psychiatrist much more than the speech-therapist, for if the dislocation has been brought about by "family, education and environment," what chance has the voice-teacher of putting things right? And if the sounds people make are the result of an inevitable 'psycho-physical conditioning,' how can it be right to produce a unity of voice and personality which never existed in the first place? In such circumstances, how can vocal training do anything other than create a voice which, firm and integrated, cannot possibly be 'natural' since the person who possesses it has been denatured by 'family, education and environment?'

What Ms. Linklater is advocating, and there is some validity in the proposition, is that through rigorous training, an actor can compensate for vocal inadequacies by eliminating the remediable problems. But then, the voice will become an instrument specifically created for the stage and therefore runs the risk of not corresponding to the 'voices' common to other people not blessed with such remedial instruction. It may produce an improved and refined voice, but to assume it will be the 'freeing of the natural voice,' the one that 'family, education and environment' have denatured, attributes to vocal training transformational possibilities that are beyond the reach of either religion, education or psychiatry.

Ms. Linklater is on much firmer ground when she refers to certain physiological faults which are aggravated by background and environment which impede our ability to speak clearly and well. By tackling the problems where they exist - in the actor's physiology - measurable improvements can be effected. "The assumption is," she writes "that there are blocks (physical and vocal) preventing the actor's creativity from being fertilized by the script, or that those blocks are preventing the free expression of what has been created. Tension is either forbidding entrance or denying exit. "Coaching removes the blocks to allow the text and the human being to begin and complete their chemical process." Which is essentially a return to the oldest idea in voice-training, namely that relaxation of the body in general and the vocal muscles in particular (plus the dissolution of psychological tension), can remove tightness in the musculature and produce freer vocal expression.

Some 'blocks' are obstacles thrown up by the material which require psychological elucidation before they can be removed. These are not vocal blocks at all, but contradictions or fallacies in the actors' approach which, by stopping him in his tracks, affect his entire interpretation as much as they do his voice. In those cases, what are diagnosed as 'vocal blocks' are merely symptoms of much larger diseases which are endemic to play-production: i.e. proceeding from a false premise, misunderstanding a scene's intention, neglecting a play's designated style, imposing characteristics on a role which are inorganic, or running counter to a director's conception.

The vocal problems that beset many actors are a symptom, not of acting- esthetics, but of the overcrowded state of the profession. It is an open secret that drama-schools, prompted by economic considerations, accept too many students and every year, more are discharged into the market-place than the market can possibly absorb. It is equally true that acting has become the one art that virtually everyone feels they can succeed at, since anyone, with no special training, is capable of speech and behavior and, superficially, that is all acting seems to require. As a result, the profession is ludicrously congested and instead of a corps of skillful actors maturing through consistent employment in a variety of roles, they are frequently edged out by hordes of unqualified questors whose number prevent the truly gifted from developing their skills. It is among this faceless horde that one invariably finds impoverished vocal techniques and, because the barriers have been lowered to admit them, valuable rehearsal-time is often wasted trying to ameliorate faults which, by all rights, should have barred such persons from stepping onto a stage in the first place. But the people who cast plays are often as untutored as the actors who turn up for cattle-calls and so one has the depressing spectacle of inadequate actors being chosen by unqualified casting-agents and obtuse directors to essay material which is usually beyond their means. This is precisely the moment when vocal-coaches and other kinds of voice-mavens are mustered into service, and the vicious cycle, unbroken, viciously circulates ad infinitum.

The dissociation of sensibility which has, for centuries, separated the voice from the body, the performance from the technical equipment which projects it, has spawned an industry as specialized and as suspect as those created by medicine. Once upon a time, General Practitioners drawing on several disciplines and a goodly amount of common sense, treated the entire human being. This was a form of holistic medicine before the term was ever invented. Today, we have endocrinologists and gynecologists, dermatologists and podiatrists, gerontologists and cardiologists, neurologists and ophthalmologists, gastro-enterologists and proctologists. All licensed specialists in their respective fields, who have parceled out the human anatomy in such a way as to suggest that each little segment is a cosmology on its own.

A similar danger is posed in the theatre where teachers now give classes in cold-reading, stage-movement, poise and relaxation, confidence-building, commercials, Tai Chi, Yoga, classical acting, stand-up comedy and aspects of voice-production which, rational as they seem to be out of context, encourage that separation of actor and instrument which can be fatal to performance.

The best vocal-coach is the sensitive director who never for a moment concentrates on vocal technique per se because he is too busy creating the three-dimensionality of the role within the context of the play. The solution to a vocal problem is to be looked for, and found, within the context of a rounded characterization and not by dividing the sounds an actor makes from everything else that constitutes his performance.

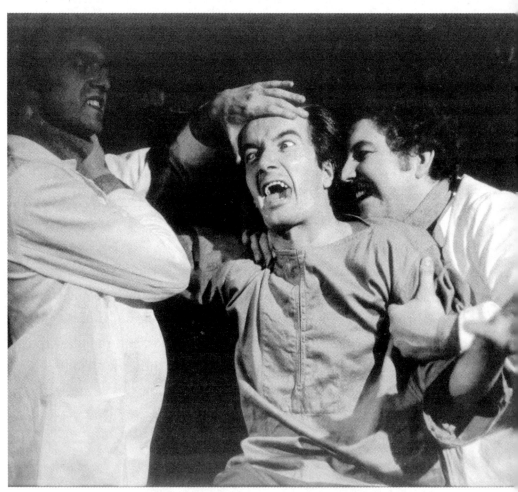

"Artaud at Rodez", Clive Merrison (center), Open Space Theatre, 1975

Donald Cooper Photography

THE INFERNAL CAFE

Scene: An infernal cafe. Empty carafes of smuggled ambrosia are littered over the table. Konstantin Stanislavsky is sipping from a wine-glass as Bertolt Brecht, holding a whiskey-bottle by the neck, plunks himself down opposite him and starts swigging. At a table nearby, Antonin Artaud, in a drug-stupor, lies with his head nestling in his arms.

STANISLAVSKY: *(Clocking Brecht's arrival)* Oh no, not again. Must you keep hounding me? Why don't you drink somewhere else?

BRECHT: Would you deny me one of the few pleasures still remaining to me?

STANISLAVSKY: You call hounding me 'a pleasure?'

BRECHT: To begrudge me that would be very mean of you, Konnie.

STANISLAVSKY: I've told you I don't like being called that.

BRECHT: Very well, Stan.

STANISLAVSKY: That's even worse. You make me sound like the dumb-half of a comedy team.

BRECHT: Oh bugger the names, Konnie. What does it matter what one is called? Names are as meaningless as everything else down here.

STANISLAVSKY: Then why do you keep pestering me?

BRECHT: *Because I, like you, cannot help being dialectical. It's in both our blood and being down here isn't going to change matters. I was thinking Konnie, of the last thing you said when we parted yesterday; about art being the only useful thing we ever had up there.*

STANISLAVSKY: *I never said any such thing. If you're going to quote me, get it right, for heaven's sake.*

BRECHT: *That's a rather pointless phrase here, isn't it?*

STANISLAVSKY: *Sorry. Force of habit. Anyway, what I said was art was the only thing that made life worth living up there. It soothed the pain.*

BRECHT: *Exactly - that's what I thought you said. But you know, soothing the pain never removed the cause of it - and your kind of art made it almost impossible to discover its root-cause. In the long run, it only made matters worse. My art, in trying to get to the bottom of things, was the only real anodyne to living. By illuminating the play-of-forces that made life miserable, it made life a little more tolerable.*

STANISLAVSKY: *Hogwash! Your 'art' never looked for answers. You had ready-made solutions provided by Marx and all those other socialist windbags. You led four generations of artists up the garden path.*

BRECHT: *I wanted one of the actor's tools to be his brains. You were arming the actor with simulations and facsimiles. I wanted to arm him with intellect and discernment.*

STANISLAVSKY: *And that's where you went very wrong, wasn't it? Because if the playwright had intellect and discernment, all the actor needed was to* speak his lines clearly and intellect and discernment would be revealed on the stage. By trying to aggrandize the actor, you confused him and ultimately crippled him. Actors work with details. They proceed step by step....

BRECHT: 'Moment to moment,' I know I've read all your books.

STANISLAVSKY: But you asked him to take an overview, to tackle the Great Issues, the Underlying Themes. That's the author's job not the actor's.

BRECHT: That's because your actor was always a mindless cretin whose head was jammed up his solar plexus. Mine was encouraged to use his brains - so that the audience would be encouraged to use theirs.

STANISLAVSKY: But it never worked did it? I mean by general consensus, it never worked. The audience was not 'alienated' by Mother Courage or your Good Woman of Setzuan. They were gripped, seized by emotion, forced to empathize. Yours was a theory perversely created to counter mine. On a theoretical realm, it had a certain interest-value, but translated into acting terms, it was paradox and contradiction. The only thing truly 'alienated' were actors, and they were alienated not by theories of verfremdung but by the contradictory results produced by your untenable ideas.

BRECHT: I grant you there was sometimes a gap between theory and practice.

STANISLAVSKY: A 'gap?' You could have shoved four centuries of literature into that 'gap.' Thousands of actors fell into that 'gap' never to be heard from again.

BRECHT: Who are you to talk? Your 'Method' reduced actors to involuntary reflexes. You took the glistening gold of dramatic art - Shakespeare,

Jonson, Marlowe, Webster - and turned it into mildewed nickels and dimes.

STANISLAVSKY; The Method certainly did that - but never the System. The System honed the talents of the finest actors of my generation and taught them how to move from realism to expressionism, from modernism to classicism. That other fellow, the American, the Method-man, he was responsible for all the reductionism. Do try to keep things in perspective.

BRECHT: But what was he but your Yankee representative? He proceeded from your principles, using your models and your terminology. He swore by your precepts. He tried to achieve your goals.

STANISLAVSKY: When I had relinquished subjectivity and monkey-see-monkey-do naturalism, he was still masturbating with emotional-memories. When I was thrusting forward with direct actions, he was still uprooting traumas from his actors' troubled childhood. Please, don't tarnish me with that brush. The two great sins of the 20th century were that no one distinguished between Communism and Stalinism and no one bothered to differentiate between the System and the Method.

BRECHT: Don't you agree that a spectator who is tensed-up with emotions and lost in his feelings cannot possibly elucidate the rights and wrongs of his social situation.

STANISLAVSKY: On the contrary, it is only after a spectator has got tensed-up with emotions and lost in his feelings, that he can recollect in tranquillity precisely why he felt the way he did. Your mistake Bertie, if I may call you that, is that you believed the public drew its conclusions in the playhouse whereas the facts are they have their experience in the playhouse, and draw their conclusions only afterwards, through retrospection.

BRECHT: *All your theatre did was to cloud spectators' minds with emotions and then draw all the conclusions for them - which is what most of modern drama still does!*

STANISLAVSKY: *Is what you are doing so very different? You had your built-in social and political biases and so when you encouraged the spectator to be 'objective,' to make up his own mind, you were already inclining him towards your values and your beliefs. It's that way with everyone. Nobody can be truly objective. Not even Chekhov was. You knew precisely where he stood on questions of the environment, landowning, serfdom, medicine, marriage, love. 'The theatre's job is to ask questions' he kept saying, but the fact is for every question he asked, he already had a pat answer and, little by little, the spectator divined it.*

BRECHT: *What you fail to see is that your theories constantly diminished the actor by forcing him to look inwards - inwards to his feelings, his memories, his past experiences - instead of outward to the world in which he was living, the society of which he was an integral part. What's the point in having an actor perfectly simulate emotions and attitudes which only make his society more reactionary and repressive. The actor, like any other citizen, has responsibilities to his fellow-man as well as to his art.*

STANISLAVSKY: *The actor who is truly an artist, cannot afford to be a politico. If he is an artist, he cannot belong to one faction rather than another, for his responsibility is to be just to all factions. That means, he must be fair - even to his enemies - sympathetic - even to his adversaries. Otherwise, he is merely a tool of prevailing policy no different from a civil servant or a party-hack.*

BRECHT: *So you don't believe the artist has a right to love justice as strongly as art - to defy bigotry and prejudice - to oppose fascism and tyranny?*

STANISLAVSKY: *As citizen, he has a right to do all these things, but as an artist, he must suspend his moral judgments lest he be unfair to his character and violate his solemn pact with the playwright.*

BRECHT: *His most solemn pact is not with the playwright but with the public. If a writer produces an unjust play - an immoral work - he is obliged to reject it; to expose it for what it is.*

STANISLAVSKY: *Then you would make the actor the arbiter of what is good or evil; to decide those delicate and complicated moral questions that have defied the efforts of the greatest philosophers and statesmen.*

BRECHT: *What's so complicated? Is it so difficult to distinguish between a good man and a tyrant, a hero or a villain?*

STANISLAVSKY: *Was Voltaire a moralist or an heretic? Was Napoleon a savior or a tyrant? Was De Sade a psychopath or a champion of sexual liberation? Depending on whom you ask, you will get some fiery answers pro and con. No, my dear Bertie, the determination of right and wrong is the most complex mystery confronting mankind - and the actor is the last person qualified to solve it. - The actor is not a moral philosopher or a dialectician; he is a technician. He employs certain muscles and mental stratagems in order to simulate effects. Like a musician, he makes the sounds dictated by the score; he follows the baton of his conductor. He is the hireling of forces greater and more knowledgeable than himself. Surely you will agree that some of the finest actors you ever knew couldn't rub two ideas together.*

BRECHT: *Some of the dullest actors I knew couldn't! Some of the finest pro-*

duced results so imbued with the glow of intellectuality that it made the scales fall from the eyes of the audience.

STANISLAVSKY: Then we have had very different kinds of experiences in the theatre. I have never learned anything in the playhouse - only had previous knowledge reaffirmed or put into question.

BRECHT: 'Put into question,' exactly! When previous knowledge is not reaffirmed but put into question, we are beginning to use the theatre for its proper purposes.

STANISLAVSKY: But reaffirmation is just as important as doubt. In fact for the young, for those people just beginning to puzzle out the muddle of existence, it is even more important to validate certain experiences, to illuminate certain connections between people and things. That is the truly instructional part of art and it has nothing to do with polemics or propaganda. It merely demonstrates to ordinary people the verities of living; the way people interact with one another; the beauty of certain feelings and the tawdriness of others.

BRECHT: Then you admit that even in your your theatre of psychology and realism you are fostering certain values and implanting certain ideas.

STANISLAVSKY: My dear Bertie, you cannot open your mouth without doing that. But there is a great difference between human revelations and premeditated beliefs; between realism and fanaticism; between implying and preaching.

BRECHT: What you have never understood Konnie, is that society is predicated on a false consciousness; on a priori ideas which it is the artist's duty to question and disturb. Your whole life was devoted to maintaining a certain artistic status quo. That is why your renegade collaborators - Meyerhold,

Vakhtangov and Michael Chekhov - were forced to abandon you. Their world-view was radically different from your own.

STANISLAVSKY: I loved them all dearly and accepted their opposition with-out malice - which wasn't always the case the other way round. But as I see it, we were all polishing different parts of the same diamond. Whatever our the-oretical differences, we were all subjects of the same Muse - albeit our worship of Her took different forms.

BRECHT: Even your metaphors are drawn from another day and age, Konnie. The best thing that ever happened to you was to expire when you did, before the whole world was transformed.

STANISLAVSKY: At last, a point on which we can both agree.

BRECHT: With all due respect, you cannot be expected to understand my rev-olutionary ideas. The theatre you worked in was the old fashioned theatre of blood and bombast bred under the Czars - then the Revolution happened, and you were plunged into a theatre of bald, propaganda. From the frying-pan into the toilet-pan, so to speak.

STANISLAVSKY: I grant you we had some dark days after the revolution - but the plays we produced, the Gogols, the Chekhovs, the Turgenevs—they have become the classic works of the modern repertoire - so it wasn't all wav-ing the red flag. Today, the Moscow Arts is still the exemplar of what is finest in.

BRECHT: - - the bourgeois theatre, yes! But there is a new actor in the world today, Konnie, and that is the man and woman who uses art to instill ideas, to foster skepticism and raise doubts. To comprehend the world in order to change it.

ARTAUD: *Goddamn it to hell, how is a fellow expected to sleep with all that rubbish flying about?!*

BRECHT: *(of Artaud who is now awake) Ah, the bohemian quarter heard from.*

ARTAUD: *"Foster skepticism" "raise doubts" "change the world." - Can you seriously be going on in that vein after the history of the past century? Your art died the same death as your politics. Communism is dead as a dodo and so are the empty polemics that informed it; the very same polemics that influenced its esthetics. Everyone now understands that social issues unrelated to the metaphysic behind them are like so many masks without faces.*

STANISLAVSKY: *Oh don't start again with all that metaphysical twaddle! Have some more absinthe and go back to sleep.*

ARTAUD: *You'd like that wouldn't you, so you wouldn't have to have your arguments demolished by good sense.*

BRECHT: *Good sense!? You're the man who wanted to toss psychology out the window - which is like throwing the baby and the bath water through the win- dowpanes!*

ARTAUD: *I never said 'toss it out the window.' On the contrary, I said blow it to bits - transcend it - for so long as it remains, we are doomed to a theatre of star-cross't lovers, secret letters, family quarrels, intrigue, infidelities, and romantic trivia.*

BRECHT: *You've practically described all the theatrical subject- matter of the past five hundred years.*

ARTAUD: Yes, but what of the next five hundred years?

STANISLAVSKY: - That's a silly thing to be discussing, if you don't mind my saying so. In the first place, none of that concerns us any longer, and in the second place, the two things that are certain to fall most rapidly out of fashion are the novelties of the present and the fantasies of the future. Stick to the verities of the past, and you'll always be fashionable.

BRECHT: Ah, the reactionary quarter heard from.

ARTAUD: (pointing to Stanislavsky) He was always a hundred years behind the time - that goes without saying. But you, (turning to Brecht), you're supposed to be the modernist and what do you do? Try to convince actors to topple governments and abolish capitalists. Do you really believe the theatre was created to be a debating society - to proliferate the social and political clichés of an election campaign? You made all of that so boring nobody even votes any more, and if you had your way, no one would go to the theatre either.

BRECHT: And you, I assume, are 'the voice of reason' - substituting cries for words, gestures for language, spectacle for drama. You who went from one loony-bin to another - chanting with Mexican Indians and brandishing the shillelagh of Saint Patrick at Jesuit priests! - Do you realize that some of the worst excrescence of modern theatrical art have been foisted in your name?!

ARTAUD: And some of the finest! Without me, there never would have been Happenings, Performance Art, deconstructed classics --- you cannot begin to talk about the modern theatre without referring to my ideas.

STANISLAVSKY: And in spite of all the rhetoric and the revolutionary theories, what is it that perseveres? Recognizable verisimilitude, comprehensible realism and the mirror reflecting back the face of man as he truly is.

BRECHT: *You're out of touch, Konnie. You left the vale of tears even before the forties began. You would never recognize the work of some of the most contemporary 'realists.' They hold the mirror up to life all right, but it is a distorting mirror and the life they reflect is recognizable only to marginal types, deviants and psychopaths.*

ARTAUD: *Your trouble Konnie --*

STANISLAVSKY: *Can't you just call me Sergeyevich.*

ARTAUD: *Your trouble Konnie is that you never understood the lamentable limitations of naturalism - in spite of the fact that your disciples Meyerhold and Vakhtangov tried to show you the error of your ways. You believed that the world was neatly bounded in a nutshell - of which the shell was 'text' and the kernel 'sub-text.' You honestly believed that once the barely concealed intentions of language were revealed, the truth was out. Consequently, your theatre, in spite of all your waffle about 'inner technique,' went no deeper than the epidermis. Our friend over here (turning to Brecht) believed that substituting theatrical illusion for the illusion of anti-illusionistic social reality would bring some kind of enhancement of perception; that by romanticizing the problems of the working-class, the middle-classes would become chastened and ultimately cease all exploitation. The nullification of his theories are splattered all over the history of the late 20th century. When the Communist icons crumbled, his esthetic theories couldn't help catching some of the flying shrapnel.*

My ideas were quiescent for about twenty-five years and when the time was ripe, came billowing out of their underground springs. The theatre was finally seen for what it was - not a replica of the external world or a political advertisement slapped over the billboards of the past - but an impenetrable psychic region capable of transmitting the most terrifying messages. The actor was neither a pretender nor a pawn in an ideological chess-game but an unleashed-force-of-nature who could delve into the mysteries which preoccupied mankind everywhere - except in the theatre, of course, where people were still fobbed off with 'whodunits' and up-market soap opera. The actor was never simply a vocal technique lodged in a physiological box, but an untapped torrent of energy whose voice was conditioned by primitive impulses; a creature more archetypal than psychological; the inhabitant of a world of dreams and myths which swirled helplessly behind his placid human nature. In short, the actor's job was not simply to simulate mankind but to recreate it in its true, existential conditions. When, in the 60s and 70s that came to be understood, the 21st century had already been inaugurated, and whatever direction it takes, it will be because of the totems and taboos I and my kind blew to smithereens.

MAROWITZ: (sauntering in) I hate to intrude in the company of my betters, but there is so much tosh being talked, I feel it incumbent upon me to say something.

STANISLAVSKY: Where did you come from?

MAROWITZ: A much later stage of development. I'm really only passing through at the moment, although no doubt I'll be with you for good before very long.

BRECHT: Have we lost all sense of exclusivity here, when we can be lectured by any two-bit, half-baked transient who feels the urge to. . . .

MAROWITZ: I'm sorry, but you see I was on hand when Mr. Artaud's revolution first surfaced and Mr. Stanislavsky's theories got renewed and extrapolated by a host of new disciples, and Mr. Brecht's theories soared then wavered then unfortunately subsided. I've seen it all, I'm afraid, and so can provide a certain perspective which, unfortunately, is denied you.

ARTAUD: Then perhaps you can explain to these old fogies just what the new theatre is really all about.

MAROWITZ: It isn't about your fuliginous theories I'm afraid - although there's no question you stirred up a real excitement in the 60s and 70s and are still cited as a great authority wherever psychological realism is being thrashed. But the fact is your works represented more of a theoretical breakthrough than a practical advance. It was fascinating in the latter part of the century to see directors such as Grotowski and groups like The Living Theatre positing some exciting alternatives to psychological realism, but Grotowski worked his way into a stylistically-strangulated cul-de-sac and The Living Theatre was more fascinating as a sociological than an artistic phenomenon. You left your mark on a handful of directors who rejigged and rethought a number of 16th and 17th century classics, but before long, it became clear that it was simply the imposition of a broad, theatricalist style which didn't truly affect content - although it effectively disguised it in many instances. The potentiality of your ideas remain current and probably will for years to come, but no one, yourself included, ever proved those theories with solid and substantial artifacts ('The Theatre Alfred Jarry' exists only as a cluster of anecdotes and 'The Cenci' left virtually no mark at all) and so you will always remain a provocateur rather than a pioneer.

And as for you Mr. Brecht, the poetry was always enthralling but more often than not, the works made statements that flatly contradicted the social-philosophy which ostensibly informed them. 'Brechtian' became an adjective which stood for minimalist sets, beautifully wrought properties, a form of narrative interrupted by song and actuality and a predisposition towards political homi-

lies. It added texture to the work of many theatres around the world but it rapidly became assimilated into the lexicon of stagecraft; another stylistic device like 'Commedia' or 'Expressionism' which could be appropriated at will - and without necessarily reflecting the philosophy from which it was derived. By the end of the century, the skepticism about your political philosophy was so wide-spread, one tended to extract the politics altogether and concentrate exclusively on the esthetics - which, as I'm sure you'll be the first to agree, made a non-sense of your weltanschauung. The trappings of The Living Newspaper and emblems of the Epic Theatre (appropriated, in the main, from Piscator) now summon up a jaded and passé theatre of the twenties. It didn't help that in the 60s and 70s, the theatres in Germany shoved Brechtian ideology down the throats of virtually everyone, causing a mass, national regurgitation - so much so that twenty years later, your country embraced the apolitical estheticism of a Robert Wilson rather than the ham-fisted propagandistic style on which it had been spoon-fed twenty years before.

And as for you Konnie, (I don't mean any disrespect but Konstantin Sergeyevitch is a bit of a mouthful), your System has the dubious distinction of having spawned the most simplistic and reductive acting-theory in the western world and one whose influence continues to attenuate and enfeeble the theatres of both America and England. You may claim that your warped American dis-ciples are responsible for producing the All American Method Actor, (an ap-palling amalgam of naturalistic tics and spasms, stuffed with mawkish emotional-memories, spouting pseudo-technical jargon, emulating Hollywood icons such as Brando, and Dean, de Niro and Pacino and worshipping an act-ing-theory because it promises, not so much artistic maturity, but super star-dom status), but this emphasis on verisimilitude and logical consistency, discouragement of classical breadth and high style and an irresistible weakness for naturalistic cliches has turned five generations of potential American giants into a succession of acting-trolls. A country that once produced actors the mag-nitude of Edwin Forrest, Junius Brutus Booth, Richard Mansfield, David

Belasco, Edwin Booth and John Barrymore now turns out a series of behav-ioral-homunculi which, in the name of Psychological Truth, simplify and fal-sify the complexities of human conduct. This onerous influence has become so pervasive it has also affected a majority of American playwrights egging them on to newer and drearier feats of vacant realism, psychological case-histories and modernistic recyclings of situations which propped up the theatre of their great-grandfathers.

Gentlemen, in one way or another, you must jointly share the responsibility for the parlous state into which the theatre has fallen.

(Pause during which Stanislavsky, Brecht and Artaud all look at one another.)

BRECHT: Isn't it always the case? Resourceful, creative people with new and exciting ideas come along and change the face of a particular art-form and no sooner do they leave the scene than 'critics' arrive to belittle their achievements.

STANISLAVSKY: I've no idea who you are, my dear friend, but I can assure you when you forsake the vale of tears, no one there will remember your name, whereas...

ARTAUD: Whereas we will be read and discussed, analyzed and lionized for as long as the theatre exists.

MAROWITZ: I don't doubt it for a moment. Read, discussed, analyzed - cer-tainly. But 'lionized?' Remember that when you came on to the scene, it was at the expense of displacing others. You Konnie, deracinated over a hundred years of false and histrionic acting-tradition in Russia. You Bertie, owed much of your acclaim to the fact that you created a dynamic alternative to Stanislavskyian realism, and m'sieur Artaud's notoriety stems from the fact that he put into question the precepts and practices of the French traditional-

ists, not to mention the naturalism of Andre Antoine and the mannered sophistication of the Boulevardiers. It is the fate of messiahs to be superseded by anti-Christs.

[Pause]

BRECHT: Shall we repair to my villa, gentlemen. There is nothing more odious than being lectured by one's inferiors.

STANISLAVSKY: You've alot to learn, sir, not only about theatre but also about good manners. - Come along gentlemen.

(STANISLAVSKY, BRECHT and ARTAUD move off leaving MAROWITZ high and dry).

*   *   *   *

STRASBERG AND THE METHOD FALLACY

The tenets of psychological realism were probed, tested and inscribed by Konstantin Stanislavsky. Like Freud, who through a rigorous self-analysis developed certain insights which were later incorporated into psycho-analysis, Stanislavsky through dissatisfaction with himself as an actor, went off to Finland in 1906 and remorselessly dissected the reasons for his inadequacy. The result was the gradual development of the Stanislavsky System, an exploration of conscious means to induce the unconscious to work freely and without hindrance in the mind and body of the actor.

Stanislavsky's acting-probes went on to the last days of his life and some of the beliefs of his last period, in the mid and late thirties, were very different from those which he first presented to the members of the Moscow Arts Theatre in the 1900s.

In 1923, the Moscow Arts Theatre made its triumphant visit to the United States. Maria Ouspenskaya and Richard Boleslavsky, members of the original company, stayed on and eventually created the American Laboratory Theatre propagating the theories and practices they had absorbed during the period of the Moscow Art's First Studio (1911-1919). It was at the American Laboratory Theatre that the 23-year old Lee Strasberg, through the aegis of Boleslavsky, first encountered the principles originally enunciated by Stanislavsky.

When the Group Theatre began in 1931, Strasberg, one of its three original directors, trained the company according to the Stanislavsky theories which had been handed down to him during the previous six years. Neither Boleslavsky nor Strasberg were aware of Stanislavsky's own revisionism in the years following the Moscow Art's visit. When Stella Adler journeyed to Paris to study with Stanislavsky, she brought back the news that much of what the Group Theatre was doing was radically different, both in procedure and emphasis, from what Stanislavsky now taught and believed. Strasberg's response to this was that his method was an adjustment of Stanislavsky's basic precepts to the conditions peculiar to the American scene. The Method, per se, was the result of that rationalization, and in 1948 when Strasberg became the Artistic Director of the Actors' Studio, it was The Method which was officially installed as the reigning doctrine. Despite certain innovations, new exercises and differences of emphasis, The Method extrapolated Stanislavsky's basic precepts, but the fundamental ideology remained the same: the actor, using his consciousness to stimulate and then regulate his unconscious, was to develop those means of expression by which true emotion, consonant with the demands of his dramatic situation, could be generated and then repeated on the stage.

The heyday of Method realism was in the 1950s when actors such as Marlon Brando, James Dean, Kim Stanley, Julie Harris, Karl Malden, Rod Steiger, Paul Newman, Ben Gazzara et al, many of them associated with the Actors' Studio, produced some striking films and plays by authors such as Arthur Miller, Tennessee Williams and William Inge. The nature of this material combined easily with the acting techniques in which the actors had already been trained. This fortuitous combination of style and content also happened sixty years before when Stanislavsky, working with the ensemble of the Moscow Arts, developed the internally-based psychologically-attuned acting-style which enabled Anton Chekhov's works to virtually come alive.

One could argue that if there had been no Stanislavsky, it is likely that Chekhov the playwright would never have surfaced - for without developing the requisite style, a dramatic work dependent on that style lacks the means through which to express itself. The disaster of the 1896 production of Chekhov's "The Sea Gull" at the Alexandrinsky Theater in St. Petersburg is perhaps the most striking example of how a play, not finding its appropriate stylistic expression, can appear mawkish and flawed. Only when it combined with the sensitive understanding of Stanislavsky and his actors did it become *"The Sea Gull."** Which points up another great truth about the theatre: often, it is the playwright who tutors the actor and leads him towards the stylistic innovation. Without Chekhov, the naturalism that the Moscow Arts so carefully cultivated would never have been able to prove itself. To a lesser extent, the same was true of the Group Theatre 'style' and the works of Clifford Odets, the Royal Court 'style' and the works of John Osborne, the Epic style of the Berliner Ensemble and the works of Bertolt Brecht. The actor is the playwright's conveyor-belt, but it is always the writer that makes that belt go round.

* It is often forgotten that it was Vladamir Nemorivich-Danchenko, the co-founder of the Moscow Arts, who persevered with Chekhov to obtain permission to revive "The Sea Gull" and that Stanislavsky had strong misgivings about its chances of success.

*   *   *   *

In 1988, Lee Strasberg's "DREAM OF PASSION: The Development of The Method" was published. Although Strasberg didn't live to complete the work, the bulk of the manuscript was largely intact when he died in 1982 and the book represents as definitive a statement on The Method from its foremost exponent that we are likely to get.

Throughout most of "DREAM OF PASSION" Strasberg reiterates the indisputable tenets of acting-training: relaxation, concentration and imagination. He either paraphrases or slightly embellishes the basic precepts laid down by Stanislavsky and includes variations contributed by Eugene Vakhtangov, one of Stanislasvky's most gifted pupils. He charts the influence of Stanislavsky from the earliest days of the Moscow Arts to the discipleship of Boleslavsky, Ouspenskaya and the lessons he himself learned as a result of training the Group Theatre ensemble. In a curious final section, he tries to obliterate the philosophic differences between Stanislavsky and Brecht and spends several paragraphs proving that, when in the '30s he and members of the Group Theatre worked on a project with Brecht in attendance, the German praised his understanding of Brechtian stagecraft and that, in a sense, there was no fundamental difference between social realism as practiced by the Group and Epic Theatre techniques as developed by the Ensemble. "The alienation effect" writes Strasberg "was not meant to deny reality." Which leads Strasberg to believe that since both disciplines are concerned with 'the real world,' they are fundamentally the same. He would like to imply that there is no disagreement between the Brechtians and the Stanislavskyians because he recognizes the flair

and uniqueness of the Brechtian stagecraft and wishes to associate The
Method with it.

Because the Brechtian actor is encouraged to achieve a certain objectivity in his work and the Method actor is occasionally asked to step
outside his three-dimensional circumference to analyze his own performance, Strasberg finds a striking parallel between the two.
Stanislavsky's exhortation to actors to look for antithetical traits in his
character - the good qualities of a bad man and the bad qualities of a
good man etc. - is misconstrued by Strasberg as a Brechtian resem-
blance. "While Stanislavskly never used the word *alienation*," he
writes,   "one of his suggestions to the actor was always to search for
the opposite - never to be satisfied with the theatrical visualization of
a character but to discover the contrary elements which help to create
the specific reality." Stanislavsky was warning the actor against caricature and one-dimensionality, suggesting a way to enrich characterization with new and subtle colors. Brecht was asking the actor to
portray the implication of his behavior, so that an audience would simultaneously see the action and its social purport. Stanislavsky's advice was in order to make the characterization more believable;
Brecht's, to encourage doubt.

Brecht, claims Strasberg, has been misunderstood by his adherents.
Ultimately, the Method and Epic Theatre share a secret solidarity - just
as he and Brecht are, in a sense, artistic kinsmen. "Brecht," he writes
"expressed his enthusiasm for our rehearsals and felt that we had been
able to work very well together. In our group, he had found hope: he
had said that his time with us had shown him that a 'revolutionary ped-
agogic theatre' was possible in America."

Nowhere does Strasberg seem to realize that the creation of true emotion and its rootedness in psychological sub-soil was anathema to Brecht; that Strasberg's theatre was the American counterpart of the 'culinary theatre' which Brecht had so forcibly turned against in his own country. That whereas Strasberg was intent on dredging up the true emotions secreted beneath recognizable social situations, Brecht was concerned to neutralize and objectify those feelings so that their social and political implications would register without emotional obfuscation. "Brecht said that the actor's identification with the character," writes Strasberg "is something to be avoided in performance. This is because Brecht feared that if the actor truly experiences, he is unable to deal with other facts demanded by the work on the character and the intentions of the scene." But it is precisely the 'intentions of the scene' which demand that the actor does *not* wholly identify with his character. It is in order to convey those intentions that Brecht urges the actor not to lose himself in his role and, by so doing, to prevent the audience from losing themselves. To keep the playwright's implications alive, it is essential that the primary motivation comes not from the character, but from what the character represents. Brecht is arguing for a topographical rather than a microscopic view of social reality. Strasberg however, cannot see beyond the reproduction of socially verifiable, three-dimensional characters.

As for Antonin Artaud, after quoting a section of the First Manifesto of the Theater of Cruelty in which Artaud describes the nature of the imagined spectacle "cries, groans, apparitions, surprises, theatricalities of all kinds, etc," Strasberg dismisses Artaud by saying: "I share Artaud's feelings for color, light and sound of Oriental theatre. However, I recognize that these aspects are historically related to social - often feudal - and religious conditions that have vanished and will not be revived. The fact is that these theatres are searching and looking for (sic) help in our Western theatres, without which they cannot find the proper representation of their own modern life. In art it is marvelous to be able to retain the master works of the past, but life goes on. If one wishes to return to some mystical womb, I understand and sympathize with the eternal need for security. But I share in and must continue to deal with the life that we live today, its struggle and its reality."

Try as he may to be *au courant*, Strasberg cannot validate a theatre which departs from 'reality' - by which he means, the psycho-social reality on which he was brought up. He cannot face the fact that there may be another reality beneath the striking verisimilitude of prevailing realism or that a theatre could conceivably deal with conflicts deeper than those that are dumped on the psychiatrist's couch. Nor does he seem to understand that what Artaud is describing is only the external trappings of the theatre he envisages and that what justifies all those external sensations is that they are in the service of exploring a consciousness deeper than the one mired in familiar social circumstance. For Strasberg, Artaud is mystical by nature and archeological by inclination. He cannot visualize an element of mystery in "the life that we live today" and is dealt with only superficially by means of psychological realism. For Strasberg, Artaud is a hothouse plant whereas Strasberg cultivates an outdoor garden full of vegetables that can be seen, picked and tasted. The man most responsible for pushing forward the frontiers of modern theatre and who declared war on the immobility of "masterpieces" is viewed by Strasberg as a man who wishes to preserve "the masterworks of the past."

But this is unfair. Strasberg, the man who was brought up worshipping Giovanni Grasso, Laurette Taylor and Jacob Ben-Ami, for whom acting, when it "was not acting" was what made it "great acting," was of the wrong generation to appreciate the metaphysical sweep of Genet, Beckett, Ionesco or Artaud. Let us accept the creature for what he was: the product of an age where the true glamour came from creating a characterization so life-like it lifted off from the stage-convention like a missile of palpitating actuality. For Strasberg, the ideal actor was the one who could feel truly and cry freely; who, at the touch of an emotional-memory, could summon up the lava of resentment, the cold ice of dread or the tear-splattering recollection of grief.

Strasberg recalls an incident when he invited some friends to share with him the majesty of Giovanni Grasso's performance as Othello which he had seen a few nights before. On the appointed night, Grasso seemed to be suffering from transmission-failure; the inspiration simply wasn't there - until, that is, a point in Act Three when, as Strasberg recalls: "He walked over to (Desdemona) as he was talking to her, put his hand on her hair and started to lift her. I have seen inspired performances, but I have not seen the moment of inspiration strike as suddenly as it did then. He touched her, and the touch seemed to create impulse. Suddenly the blood rushed into Grasso's face; his eyes distended. This was acting: this was real - real blood, real bursting of blood vessels. From that moment on, his face, his whole body and his entire performance changed. I sat upright in my chair, willing to take bows. The great actor had suddenly proved that he *was* a great Actor."

For Strasberg, the proof of Grasso's greatness was that he managed to produce a startling, emotional effect - one that brought "real blood, - real bursting of blood vessels." Even in his earliest days, when as a boy he watched performances of Yiddish theater on the lower east side of New York, Strasberg was helplessly seduced by the detonation of strong emotions; the 'big moment,' the dynamic effect, the intrusion of 'real life' into the fictional construct of the stage.

For Strasberg, conjuring up a physiological truth is the be-all and end-all of art. This emotional release is always hailed as an acting-success - in spite of the fact that it is rarely transferred into the context of a play in which it has to be controlled, modulated or conceivably, even suppressed. Nor does Strasberg seem to understand that what makes such moments effective in a drama is not necessarily their verifiable truthfulness but the fact that they connect up with a narrative strand in the audience's imagination and it is that narrative connection which often produces the dramatic effect. Romeo, mistakenly believing Juliet to be dead, takes the poisoned potion thinking it will unite him with his beloved. It is because we know that he will perish by drinking it and that Juliet is still alive that his action creates in us such an overwhelming sense of poignancy. The actor, realistically expiring from poison, is irrelevant to the dramatic impact. It is the *idea* of what is happening that is compelling; not the act itself; the twist of the plot, not the accuracy of the actor's physiological reaction to drinking the potion. Which is why it is often possible to be moved by such moments even in amateur productions where actors lack polish and experience.

The clinical re-creation of reality is often one of the greatest turn-offs on the stage. Since a play is essentially a letter directed to our imaginations, we resent a drama which forces us to proofread its contents and check its grammar. The truth we are hungering for is not the recreated truth of life, but the refined and heightened truth which is what justifies its formulation as art. It is true that implausible actions and unconvincing behavior violate our appreciation of what is being presented. But more often, it is the intrusion of unadorned, life-based realism which shatters our illusion. Until the sandbag falls from out of the flies or the actual cup inadvertently smashes in the actor's hands, we are prepared to believe we are in a 14th century castle or a 19th century drawing-room. Often it is the arrival of the naked truth which spoils our appreciation of the artistic lie.

Strasberg's fundamental fallacy is to believe that life can be transferred wholesale into art and that art will always benefit from the transaction.

All of Strasberg's exercises are obsessively concerned with recreating real conditions in the unreal circumstances of art. He encourages the actor to use imaginary objects in order to experience the reality of the actual objects before they arrive. "Once the actor learns how his senses function when that object is present, he then learns to recreate these reactions and responses when the object is not present." But the sense of the real object is never exactly the same as the imaginary one. The impression of the object may change with atmospheric conditions, with the speed or slowness with which it is offered, with the brusqueness or gentleness with which it is received. A cigarette passed to an actor by a character who is trying to induce him to light up despite his resolution to quit smoking, is not the same as an imaginary cigarette mimed in an acting-exercise. The *real* cigarette in the *real* context has a reality which can only be experienced within the context of a scene in which the actual object represents a *real* threat. And since the sense of touch is virtually automatic, how is the actor helped by trying to imagine what, in any case, he cannot fail to experience in the actual situation? Only in mime-plays is it useful to simulate the weight, feel and texture of an object that does not tangibly exist.

But the actor is developing his sense-memory, Strasberg would answer. But that is like asking an actor to practice his sense of smell or exercise the reflexes of his auditory nerve. Those senses are always operative in the actor and require no special training. What *does* need work is mastery of the prop; a sense of its weight and balance; its tendency to slip out of one's hands or become damp or unmanageable. That is knowledge which can only be gained by dealing, in a tactile way, with the real object and not its imaginary substitute.

In the theatre, the actor's senses are sharpened not by reflection but by being challenged by other actors exercising *their* senses. Someone throws you an object which you have to catch; a punch that you have to deflect; a sound you didn't expect. It is the interaction of senses which sharpens your own - not their recollection in isolation.

Even in so basic an area as relaxation, Strasberg's suggestions are misguided. The actor should sit in a chair, he suggests that "affords him some comfort and support for his body. Check each area of (the actor's) body for presence of tension." As for mental tension, "All that is necessary to achieve relaxation is to try to release the energy, to feel the energy oozing out of this area. Though this may sound difficult, it is easy to do." And again, "all one needs to do to achieve relaxation there (around the bridge of the nose) is to permit the eyes to close a little bit, just as one does when going to sleep, to allow the energy too ooze out."

This is tantamount to telling the actor that the best way to relax is to "just relax". But it has been demonstrated time and time again, that the best way to discharge tensions is through a highly energetic, full-body work-out which involves sounds and movements; a work-out similar to a dancer's limbering but specifically geared to the needs of the actor. After a strenuous thirty minute physical session which tones up the imagination as well as the muscles, the psyche as well as the soma, the actor is virtually tension-free. Although as soon as he begins to work on scenes or acting-exercises, the tension can immediately return — for essentially, the source of tension is not in the body but in the brain and the profoundest relaxation will vanish as the actor re-experiences a hurdle he cannot jump or a conflict he does not understand.

Strasberg also fails to make the essential distinction between circumstantial tension and armoring. In the case of the former, the presence of a 'block' brought about by fear or anxiety can be isolated and removed — usually through work-out and occasionally, massage. But some actors possess biological tension which is literally built in to their bodies through childhood or early adolescent traumas; this is what produces the body-armor which was one of Wilhelm Reich's most significant discoveries. In those cases, only the psychotherapist is of any real help and depth-analysis, and not acting-training, is what is called for. But for normal, circumstantial tension, a full-body work-out which localizes various sets of muscles and lubricates all the working parts of the body, is still the best antidote.

In challenging roles, the actor is often asked to express intensely felt emotions. Strasberg's recipe here is emotional memory; the concentrated recreation of incidents from the actor's past which can powerfully re-evoke what was once intensely experienced. In an exercise situation, this can produce some astounding results. In a performance situation, it can effectively shatter the emotional infra-structure of a character's development.

The introduction of alien memories into a role in order to 'make' an emotional climax is the equivalent of the steroid-injections certain athletes take to artificially bolster their musculature. The arbitrariness of such a device invariably intrudes into the mental film-track running in the actor's mind and clogs the relevant mental imagery with alien matter. Emotional memories are not interchangeable. The death of a pet hamster in adolescence is not qualitatively the same as that attending the death of a monarch or a parent, and in attempting to conjure up an alien setting and a different time-frame, the actor's mind necessarily departs from the given circumstances which should be feeding the requisite feelings. In his later teachings, Stanislavsky virtually abandoned emotional-memory - concentrating instead on total immersion in immediate actions. Through these, he believed, the relevant emotions would be summoned up, and he recognized the dangers of breaking the emotional continuity of a character's concentration by intruding moods or incidents which were not germane.

But for Strasberg, emotional memory was not so much a tool as a parlor trick and one that almost any actor could accomplish. The irony, which I discovered in my own experiments with this exercise, was that often the actors who were most effective in conjuring up effective emotional memories were frequently the least talented. For the persons most susceptible to the surge of traumatic memories are invariably the most neurotic and troubled. Their success in this exercise has more to do with their wracked backgrounds than any interpretative skills they may possess. And then, of course, there are the highly sensitive, often socially inhibited, actors who resent the fact that highly personal matter is being dredged out of their past. It was often these more discerning actors, the ones who raised ethical objections to the exercises, who never needed them in the first place in order to produce motivated results. It is hard to consider the whole question of Strasberg's self-exploratory approach without drawing the conclusion that, apart from a handful of talented adherents, it is a discipline which appeals mostly to gullible and neurotic people who crave doctrine the way the religiously-naive crave the dogma of bogus tele-evangelists.

*   *   *   *

There is yet another paradox in The Method and one of the most surprising.

Because the emphasis is so entirely on the actor's inner state, The Method unwittingly militates against the player-to-player contact which is where deeply-researched personal work, if it has to have any value, needs to be minted.

An actor's performance grows in a soil that is collectively culti-vated. His finest moments are contingent upon and return to the work of the ensemble of actors with whom he is working. But Strasberg's approach encourages the actor to solve his problems in isolation - so much so that a doctrinaire Method actor will sometimes refuse to dis-cuss a scene with his playing-partner, preferring instead to let his feel-ings spontaneously combust during the course of the performance. Consequently, Method actors are very easy to pick out in almost any cast. They are the persons who are generating results on their own. The validation of those results are the actors' own feeling of veracity about what is being created, without reference to the fact that a per-sonal truth which doesn't merge with the collective truthfulness is, by dint of that dissociation, subversive to the scene.

The Method actor is isolated in two ways. First of all, he or she is often a class-junky encouraged in perpetual workshop situations to work in fragments, on exercises and emotional memories out of context. The material itself is almost always partial since acting-classes do not produce plays, but merely scenes or moments from plays. Having cultivated singularity in the acting-class, the performer brings that attitude of mind into a play when he or she is actually cast. The 'training' has conditioned the actor to solve personal problems on his or her own and the practice continues in the collective situation despite the fact that the priority is now upon the group rather than the individual. This is also why doctrinaire Method actors cannot live compatibly with a director for in their mind, the struggle to achieve the pristine emotional purity of certain beats is *their own* concern, and no one else's. As a result, such actors develop a subtly evasive attitude in regard to their directors. They *appear* to collaborate but cannot break the habit of working apart. It is one of the Method's greatest ironies that a theory of acting spawned by a magnificent ensemble, the Group Theatre, and inspired by an even more magnificent ensemble, the Moscow Arts, winds up creating detachment rather than collaboration. But it is well known that acting-dynamics untested in performance-situations are dangerously deceptive. Here Strasberg's ill-fated Actor's Studio production of Chekhov's 'The Three Sisters' forcibly comes to mind. If ever one needed a living demonstration of actors out of sync with one another, this was it. All the relevant Method principles were assiduously applied, but Chekhov never came alive. The operation was a success but the patient died.

*   *   *   *

It is the Method's intractability in regard to Shakespeare and the classics where its fundamental shortcomings are most clearly revealed. Why does the doctrinaire Method approach, which is unquestionably effective with modern plays, fail so miserably with classical works?

A classic is more than the sum total of its characters and situations. It inhabits a time-frame which conditions both the thoughts and speech of its characters. It is contained in a philosophic framework, different from our own which, in most instances, can bridge the past with the present but nevertheless, never loses its original stylistic chararacter. To bring it from its own time-frame into our own, an imaginative leap is required on the part of actors and directors. Like vintage wine being poured from old bottles into new, the process needs delicate handling so that the transfer from one vessel to the other will be successful. We acknowledge that a classic's original style is different from the conduct and behavior of its contemporary interpreters, but we recognize that there are enough parallels to make such a transfer perfectly feasible, and where it is not feasible, we are prepared to respect the original work and attempt to 'revive' it on its own terms. The key to all of these transfers is an understanding of the work's original style, so that in modifying, altering or even departing from that style, we are still dealing with the ideological content which gave the original work its value.

The Method's style is, as it were, built-in. Its DNA spawned by Stanislavsky and inherited by Strasberg, has inescapable characteristics - just as biological DNA has basic and inescapable genetic components. It seeks to strike a balance between the actor's sense of reality and the characters,' no matter what period-differences may exist. The actor translates his character's thoughts and emotions through his own, the assumption always being that human nature is constant and what was essentially true for one century remains constant for succeeding generations.

But of course, history shows us that is not the case. That, for example, there were certain class-distinctions in earlier centuries which no longer apply today and so the resultant behavior has to be either modified or altered. We know that in the 17th century, people's ideas about religion and their relation to the deity were different from our own; that a belief-system like the Chain of Being, for instance, cannot possibly apply to a contemporary sensibility where atheism, agnosticism and even heresy are legitimate modes of thought.

Knowing these things and trying to make sense of them in a modern context involves very delicate adaptations to the language and behavioral-life of another time. It is not a matter of pulling a switch from Period to Modern but of evolving a contemporary style which will permit the original style to be refashioned without violating those elements which made it worth preserving in the first place. A style goes in search of a style; a text looks for connotations and inferences which, acknowledging its original meaning, will make it meaningful again in our own time.

Because The Method's style is, as I say, built-in and because it encourages the personal styles of the actors employing it to suffuse the work, the whole question of stylistic integrity is virtually ignored. Like a steamroller, The Method flattens the classic and then tacitly demands that it rise up and become as vertical as it was before. If the classic is written in blank verse, The Method actor, imposing the rhythms which seem truest to his nature - rather than *its* nature - assumes it will assimilate whatever rhythm he chooses to give it; poetry gets prosified, historicity is contemporized. Because he divines certain social insights which, in his mind, give it contemporary relevance, he forces it out of its britches and waistcoat and into jeans and t-shirts. The assumption is always the same: I can make sense of this old work by trickling it through the sieve of my modern sensibility. I *understand* Hamlet's vacillation (I too have found it hard to make up my mind about returning to school or staying at home), Macbeth's ambition (I once wanted to be president of the company and schemed to get rid of a rival), Othello's jealousy (I once thought this bitch was two-timing me and went slightly off my rocker), Angelo's duplicity (I once wanted this girl to sleep with me in return for getting her brother a cushy job with the firm). In a thousand minuscule different ways, the grandeur and size of Shakespeare's characters are whittled down to what Method actors conceive as viable parallels and then played in such a way as to utterly obliterate their intrinsic meaning. In the trade-off (in which the classic is consistently shortchanged), the actor substitutes behaviorism for elegance, contemporary speech-patterns for literary constructs and verisimilitude for period style.

By weighing the veracity of its expression on the scale of truthful personal feeling, the Method actor blithely ignores the fact that the classic's truth inhabits a different imaginary realm and is couched in a style antithetical to his own. The British actor assiduously tries to recreate the period conditions of the 16th, 17th and 18th centuries; he learns how to move 'according to the costume' and to speak in the accents of the time but often, in failing to translate the sensibility of the former time into the present, he produces only archeological results.

The Method Actor, neglects all those academic considerations and heads straight for the expression of the parallel truth; the meaning of the play as he comprehends it in 20th century thought-and-speech patterns.

By preserving the style of the original, The British actor, if he can coalesce a modern sensibility and a period structure, has an opportunity to bring the classic imaginatively to life. The Method actor, in believing that his style is interchangeable with that of the original, winds up just spinning his wheels. Confronted with the artificiality of Congreve or Wycherley, he proffers realism - or, often what is worse, false mannerism; his distorted caricature of 18th century behavior replete with handkerchiefs, snuff-boxes, muffs and fans. By assuming that a rake is just an old-styled 'make-out man' and a dandy merely the prototype of a drag-queen, he imposes familiar social types onto an author's character rendering the originals *un*recognizable. Proceeding from Strasbergian principles, he is looking for the 'truth of the character,' but through the labyrinths of his *inner* truth and, in so doing, is blind to the fact that in artificial comedy, the truth lies not in psychic emanations, but in the play's artifice; in Shakespeare, not in topical impositions, but in the bedrock of the play's theme, structure and text. The Method's own style is so loaded down with realistic shibboleths, it is incapable of recognizing the extravagance and paradox of works in which the surface *is* the substance.

Nor is this failing limited to the works of earlier centuries, for the fact is modern realism has just as many different facades as those found in the plays of Shakespeare or Marlowe, Webster or Fletcher, Vanbrugh or Etheredge. The stylishness of Noel Coward or Philip Barry, S.N. Behrman or Edward Albee demand a mode of realism different from what one might associate with Clifford Odets, Sidney Kingsley or Arthur Miller. Stanislavsky understood, particularly in his later years, that 'truthful behavior' could not be entirely self-referential, but had to be truthful to the style of the playwright. By allowing the nature of the material to dictate the style of the acting, (and thereby rationalize its contradictions and inconsistencies), the actor was acknowledging the fact that truth was pluralistic and not monolithic. That, in a sense, every play worth staging possessed its own 'acting-system' and that it could be discovered only by being approached openly and without *a priori* principles and rigid methodologies.

I have probably gone too far in railing against Strasberg and The Method, so let me judiciously backtrack.

Strasberg's greatest legacy to us is that he recognized the virtues contained in Stanislavsky's thought, and the tenets of what he called the System are as valid today as they were when Stanislavsky first defined them. As Harold Clurman pointed out, it is preposterous to attack 'grammar' and grammar is precisely what Stanislavsky offers: a syntax and a structure by which characters can be formulated and developed and a series of techniques which can help actors produce the free flow and lucid effects which, when they organically interact, virtually simulate inspiration. It is the emphases and false hypotheses of The Method which have derailed Stanislavsky's central integrity; which, instead of widening out their possibilities, have narrowed them down.

There are certain truths both in Stanislavsky and Strasberg which are esthetically indisputable. The theories evolved as an antidote to bombast and artificiality and it was the removal of those cloying traits which hauled acting into the 20th century. But we are now on the brink of the 21st century and it is time to reappraise the rigidities and obsolescence which now impede their effectiveness. It is time to analyze and expunge the limitations of a technique which is no longer suited to the needs of a constantly innovating modern theatre. Not by scrapping everything that has gone before but by judiciously adding and amending what will be most useful for the future.

It always struck me as significant that the most exciting departures from realism were produced by Meyerhold, Vakhtangov and Michael Chekhov, the very directors and actors that Stanislavsky nurtured. Therein lies the secret of proper artistic development. Having drunk from the fount of the master, the disciples go off to create their own watering-holes. It is from the nutrients of realism that Theatricalism, Expressionism, Surrealism and every other 'ism' has developed. When the water of the fountain is clear and not spiced with one flavor or another, it can quench any number of thirsts.

"Tooth of Crime", Open Space Theatre, 1974

Donald Cooper Photography

THE PARADOX OF THE ACTOR

"In all the activities of life," Aldous Huxley wrote "from the most trivial to the most important, the secret proficiency lies in an ability to combine two seemingly incompatible states - a state of maximum activity and a state of maximum relaxation."

Huxley was dealing with philosophical matters but his words apply, without alteration, to the paradox of the actor. When true acting happens, it too combines 'maximum activity' and 'maximum relaxation.'

In the same essay, "The Education of an Amphibian", Huxley goes on to dismantle Descartes' dictum Cogito ergo sum - 'I think therefore I am,' arguing that it is only when the conscious mind is unclenched that the "indwelling intelligences" of the inner self can take over, and only then that the ego is "prevented from succumbing to its old bad habits" and "eclipsing the inner lights."

Huxley, a Vedantist and a mystic, is concerned with larger subjects than characterization and acting inspiration. He is writing about the conduct of life grounded upon social and spiritual predicates. But his key-point curiously intersects with the problem of the actor. Beyond the ego and beneath the id, there is a territory from which astounding insights can be dredged up to the world above, and if the actor finds a way to shuttle from one to the other, he can confer an entirely new dimension to what occurs on a stage.

Diderot's "Paradoxe Sur le Comdian" concerned itself with an artificial distinction: actors who yielded to feeling and those that kept it under strict control. Any practicing actor could have told him that virtually every performance represents a compromise between both states; that an actor is constantly fluctuating between being "lost in his role" and consciously guiding it, and that this 'neither-nor' state creates a sensibility which is not subject to one doctrine or the other. There never was an actor who didn't technically keep his emotions in check and occasionally toss himself into their whirlpool.

The real 'paradox' of the actor has less to do with conscious or unconscious emotion and very much more to do with the plane on which he decides to pitch his performance. If he opts for surface reality, the 'paradox' is that he quickly becomes implausible because 'natural behavior,' reproduced in the unnatural environs of a stage, only emphasizes the disparity between life and art. If he opts for more radical, expressionist behavior which, for example, attempts to externalize internal states, he stands in danger of becoming pretentious and incomprehensible. (On the one hand, the Boulevard; on the other, the murky pit of the Avant-Garde). And yet, directors as dissimilar as Grotowski, Kantor, Brook and The Becks have achieved startling results in the latter category, and there is a great slew of main stem actors who, far from sacrificing plausibility in realistic roles, have, with power and subtlety, triumphed in them. Obviously there is a golden mean somewhere.

Diderot notwithstanding, there are in fact numerous paradoxes in the theatre besides the one he made the subject of his stimulating discourse in 1773. First, there is the paradoxical act of 'public privacy' so often alluded to by Stanislavsky, then there is the paradox of endlessly repeating lines and movements to give the impression that they are occurring for the first time; the paradox of using one's own personality to project another and yet acknowledging, to oneself and one's public, that though the two are inseparable, the act of performance is intended to separate them - to project the mask and not the face.

Another paradox is that the actor is portraying character and situation, not for their own sake but as a means of insinuating some implicit idea that a playwright has concocted and a director interpreted. That a physical performance is an embodiment of a notion, an attitude, a criticism or a warning of which it is merely the pretext.

There is also a paradox in the tacit contract that exists between the actor and his public; the assumption, for example, that the representation of human conduct on stage in some way parallels the public's own experience when in fact it is a compression, synthesis and sometimes distortion of those events which we attribute to 'real life.' A mirror held up to Nature reflects only that circumscribed in the frame which contains the glass. Esthetically speaking, the dimensions of the frame are everything. And yet what we look for in the theatre is some expanded and all-inclusive version of reality. Not a microscopic reduction of life or a mirrored reflection of its outward show, but something larger and more synthesizing than life.

When we examine post modernist trends in the theatre, the paradoxes multiply even further.

In various forms of Performance Art where dramatic works are deconstructed, freed from narrative continuity or juxtaposed with contradictory events or deliberate acts of distortion, the assumption is still that artists are presenting some version of a generally shared experience, or leastways one based on a work that exists in some previous,

more linear form. When Mabou Mines, for example, performs its frac-
tured version of Chekhov's "The Three Sisters" in a series of arbitrary
segments with characters very far removed from those described by the
author and in a style which deliberately alienates the content of the play,
the paradox is that without the Chekhovian starting-point and everything we now know and feel about "The Three Sisters" after some
ninety-seven years, there would be no basis for the production. We are
being presented with a radical reorganization of a work which, if we are
to assess it in any way at all, must in some way be referred back to the
original but, paradoxically, the original has been swallowed up in the re-
cension and the more we look for it, the less we will experience the new
work to which it has given birth. Perhaps the greatest paradox in the
theatre is that the passage of time and the social transformations of the
theatregoing public make it impossible literally to 'revive' any work,
and that the word 'revival' itself is a semantic mockery for what happens
to an old work presented in a new era to a gathering of people who view
it with an entirely different social and psychological mind-set.

The theatre is, quintessentially, the art of contradiction and since
contradiction is the inescapable condition of life, we learn more about
the latter from the former than from almost any other medium. It is
also the key to producing revelatory acting effects. Recognition-scenes,
denouements, the unravelling of mysteries, the discovery of concealed
facts: all theatre tends in these directions and the same elements can be
found in performance. The text yields to the sub-text, the sub-text to
the ur-text. As a play progresses, we discover a character's hidden motives, then the character discovers the roots of his own motives or those
of others who have challenged or opposed him, and stage by stage, we
shear away the layers of concealment with which society and psychology have obfuscated our strongest needs and deepest drives.

In the old theatre, the theatre of melodrama and the early theatre of realism, a playgoing experience was predicated on one central revelation; a discovery that three quarters of the play was created to camouflage. The peasant was really a prince; the virtuous man really a scoundrel; the maligned victim really a saint. In the so-called, modern theatre, the revelations are less particularized, the morality more ambiguous, the outcomes more open to different interpretations. In our post modernist age, we are more concerned with the processes beneath both character and action than we are with either in their own right. We experience the fragmentation of the theatre and the strands that constitute character in order to reassemble both for ourselves. Our intellect is much more participatory; our aversion to foregone conclusions much more intense.

The material dredged up by the actor correlates with that of his character, but because we are more in touch with the physical presence of the interpreters, the original character is suffused by the character of the actor. Burbage's Macbeth, Kean's Othello, Bernhardt's Phaedre, Barrymore's Hamlet, Oliver's Richard III have traveled very far from their author's original conceptions, and yet we can experience the author's intentions only through such interpreters.

The diversity of those actors' performances, over a period of centuries, gives a classic a sense of accumulated force which is central to our theatregoing experience, but it is so much a fusion of then-and-now, so cumulative an experience, that we can never conclusively disentangle our contemporary impressions from those posited in the original play by its original author. We rationalize this paradox by saying that a classic is supposed to speak differently to different generations, but we never analyze precisely what earlier exponents have bequeathed to later ones or how similar or different they may be from one another, or to what extent our feelings are the result of what a modern actor has unconsciously assimilated from his predecessors. Exposing oneself to a classic is like stepping into a time-machine that shuttles endlessly between the present and the past. No matter how modern we may believe it to be, it reverberates with echoes from the near and far distant past.

The unifying thread in all these paradoxes is that theatre is a way of both stopping and extending time; an action which is simultaneously existential and past. An actor stepping on stage in a classic is, in equal measure, immediate and archival. And this same dynamic applies to what an actor is trying to do: creating the realistically-based, behavioral moment and the conscious and unconscious energies which swirl beneath it. The known and the precognitive in tandem. The newly-minted modern effect and those buried layers of antiquity which lie beneath its immediacy.

Grumpy and slightly frustrated with things being neither one thing nor the other, one is tempted to say, as with Lord Caversham in "An Ideal Husband:" "That is a paradox, sir. I hate paradoxes."

THE COMPULSIVE NEED FOR LOVE

"Your trouble," said the actress with a quaver in her voice, "is that you just don't know how to give any love!"

It was a heartfelt indictment, it hurt and I guess it was true. The work had been marked by all the usual ups-and-downs of the rehearsal cycle. Initial choices were abandoned or proved fruitless; others were adopted in their stead. I was morose, but persevered; she was crestfallen, but kept trying. Eventually, something began to bud, ultimately to flower. We had both watched it happen. We had seen 'something' grow miraculously out of 'nothing;' a wisp of a new idea hatched on the funeral pyre of a dozen expired ideas suddenly took on heat and light and we both sensed there was a way out of the darkness; a glimmer that looked tantalizingly like light at the end of the tunnel.

In my folly, I thought the realization, the unexpected growth which we had mutually experienced, was so self-evident, so unquestionable, nothing more needed to be said. I was wrong. What was needed on her part was a demonstrable show of gratitude, an affirmation of her talent, her fortitude, her ability to rise phoenix-like from the ashes of barren moments and manifest failure. What she wanted and what she needed was 'love' - for at base, the hunger for that affirmation was nothing less.

It was not deliberately withheld. It was simply that the mutual turmoil we had undergone was so apparent to both of us and its reversal so joyously unexpected, it never occurred to me that overt acknowledgment needed to be made. She, moreso than anyone else, knew how magnificently she had succeeded and, because I watched every wriggle of torment and was present through every paralytic frustration, I assumed that she understood that I understood the significance of what we had jointly brought about. She didn't, and what she took as coldness soured our relationship forever after.

The actors' compulsive need for love is rooted in something much deeper than the human fellowship of play-production. It is an aching thirst which remains unquenched no matter how often refreshed. It is the hidden motor which, in their earliest years, propels young men and women to the stage and is nourished and refueled every time the audience breaks out into applause. It is the fulfillment of whatever endocrinal need it is that makes actors want to feel the breath of their public, the emanation of their body heat, the systole and diastole of their shared breathing, and the clatter of their unanimous approval. It is what the actor lives for, and recognizing the banality of that observation in no way diminishes its urgency. It is not merely approval, it is not simply recognition of effort, it is the public avowal of a constantly doubted sense of self-worth which validates their personal anguish and professional suffering. It is also the neurotic's coronation and the psychotic's ultimate moment of triumph.

For in the act of creation, the compulsive need for love is the equivalent of Joan of Arc's need for immolation. When she listened to her voices, championed her Dauphin and led her troops, she was 'playing her actions' but when she embraced the stake, she threw herself into her delirium. The very delirium that underlay the energy with which she originally 'played her actions.'

The energy that feeds the actor's ego, that works for triumph and canonization instead of the steady flow of purposeful activity, is a liability and not an asset. It is the desire to be 'loved for his art' rather than allowing that art to realize its fullest potential. It is an impulse of the Super-Ego in a field where the Unconscious delivers the greatest riches. It grows from the need to be approved not for one's skills but for one's self. It is an intrusion of narcissism by means of which the inward-look supplants the outward glance.

A director is constantly turning on and shutting off the faucet of his affections in order to elicit results from his company. There are some actors who can only function within the cocoon of a director's good graces. They are the weaker actors. The stronger ones derive their confidence from the certainty of their own powers. They use the director mainly as a kind of barometer to gauge the efficacy of their work. They know that an absence of commentary almost always means they are on the right track, and that relentless probing and analysis infers the existence of unsolved problems. The director is so preoccupied with the unraveling of intractable matter that he is tacitly grateful for those moments in which the actor's taste and skill are getting on with the job at hand. There is a lunatic assumption in the profession that a director is obliged to direct every moment of a production whereas in fact, if he has cast the play judiciously, the casting itself accounts for a large percentage of what falls readily into place. It is the interstices, the places between the character's reach and the actor's grasp, that mainly monopolize him; the arduous, impenetrable, unattainable moments that defy simple solutions and pat answers. In the midst of baffling enigmas and torturous contradictions, the director is as strung out as the actor -

both striving to find a sense of direction by which they can resolve what appear to be insoluble dilemmas.

To expect love and affirmation at such times is like expecting two mountain-climbers teetering on a rock-face to stop and give each other a congratulatory hug just before achieving the summit. The actor and the director, to pursue the simile, are indeed roped together, dependent on each other's fortitude to reach a designated point. The director, unless he is a detached observer (which virtually nullifies his function as a director) is part-and-parcel of the actor's effort to solve the problems thrown up by the play. He is not the trainer egging on the fighter from the sidelines; he is in the ring, as bruised and bloody as either of the combatants.

The actor's need to be loved is akin to the child's need to be coddled and reassured - whether reassurance is justified or not. And we all know what happens when children get false assurances. They are made so vulnerable that when they encounter real conflict, they simply fall apart. The child who believes he is invincible and is then trounced by an oversized bully doesn't thank the parents who filled him with false confidence. A few lessons in judo or karate would have been more beneficial than constantly-bestowed hugs and kisses.

The emotional approval that actors long for is both understandable and available, but it is bestowed not by a surrogate father-figure called a director, but by the public which validates actors' choices and confirms the truth of what they themselves have found to be true in the play. Is there anything more disorientating and humiliating than an actor, buoyed up with false confidence by a director, suddenly obliged to confront pathetic failure at the hands of public and critics? One can argue that the director's encouragement gave him the strength to play confidently in the first place, but one can just as easily argue that because of his weakness and frailty, he was led into a false paradise where all critical objectivity was suspended and the agonies of creation replaced by ego-emoluments.

The strong actor uses the director as a sounding-board to confirm his own instincts. He doesn't seek reassurance. He reassures himself. The weak actor, unable to achieve a perspective on himself other than what is conveyed by others, can view himself only in the reflection thrown back by his director. It is dependency disguised as collaboration.

The director is the resident critic of the production; the actor, the inescapable object of his criticism. The source of the criticism stems from those actors' impulses which stray from or deny the conception of the play as envisaged by the director. Not always, for sometimes the actor, with unfailing instincts, finds values that never occurred to the director and which, if he is sensible, the director will gratefully acknowledge and promptly appropriate. But more often, the director is piloting the actor into latitudes and longitudes which belong to his own navigational grasp of the work. To do so successfully, he is obliged to rationalize his original choices and alter, modify or reverse those of the actor which run counter to them. Knowing that what the actor independently finds for himself will most benefit his mise-en-scene, the director cunningly sets traps for the actor, hoping he will slip into the choices he has consciously set out for him. When the actor sidesteps these traps, when he goes 'his own way' and that 'way' appears to be counter to the grain of the work, the director quietly panics. He has arranged every locomotive to arrive at a prearranged terminus and the appearance of a wild engine threatens a calamitous pile-up. The director wheedles, cajoles, theorizes and manipulates in order to bring the actor back on track and the brunt of his criticism stems from the fact that the actor is resisting the gravitational tug of his interpretation.

The actor, unless he subscribes to the timetable laid out by the director and is amenable to arriving at the prescribed destination, clings to his own particular diversion, sees it as the more correct route and actually prefers his destination to that of the director's. It is at that point that conflict enters into their working relationship. The assumption is that the actor is 'taking direction' - the reality is that he is cleaving to his own. How can one person - a director - compel the intonations, intentions and motions of another - the actor - when each is proceeding from a different standpoint towards a different goal? It is in the subtle, often unarticulated, discord that runs beneath this contradiction that productions rapidly collapse. The official explanation is usually attributed to "artistic differences" and, banal as the phrase may be, it is almost always perfectly accurate. An "artistic difference" is the inevitable consequence of incompatible ideas struggling for dominance within the context of the same production and resignation or dismissal is an honorable solution to these problems. Economic considerations to one side, the alternative to separation is corruption of the play and disaster to all concerned.

Which ideas should predominate? One is tempted to say 'the best,' but then who is the arbiter of that? In the professional theatre as constituted in the western world, the director's prerogative is expected to hold sway, and usually does. But I have known many productions where the irrepressible tendency of a self-willed actor has swept a production into a dangerous and innovative direction which, if followed, could have produced startling results - only to have it subdued and routinized by the insistence of a director bent on realizing his original blueprints. There is no formulaic answer to that question. The current dispensation demands that the director's conception, banal and predictable as it may be, must prevail. But in those instances where hierarchy is suspended and ensemble principles are given free play, a result is possible which transcends the specifications of any blueprint, no matter how grandly conceived. I understand that the innovative French Canadian director Robert Le Page gives his actors an exceptionally wide brief as does the British director Declan Mulholland. So does Peter Brook and Jorge Lavelli. On the other hand, the despotism of Vsovolod Meyerhold and Peter Stein have produced equally impressive results.

But it is criticism, the persuasion of actors along a preordained directorial route, that is the production's primary mechanism. Sometimes that criticism is couched in gentle and amiable terms; sometimes it is blunt and sometimes, harshly personalized. But whatever form it takes, it is the actor being forced to adapt himself to instructions which issue from the director presumably at the behest of the play. A rehearsal-period is an unbroken wave of criticism from beginning to end; even the instructions to rise or sit, move or stand still are gestures arising from a directorial conception of the whole and belong to the gradually evolving design shaping inside a director's head.

Let's put this even more succinctly. The director is telling the actor what to do, how to do it and, in best of all possible worlds, why it needs to be done as he says. The actor is not a pawn or a flunky and when his celebrity is greater than the director's, he virtually directs himself with the alleged director simply going through the motions. But in most cases, the director is the authority from which final decisions emanate. During the course of rehearsals, the actor develops a modus operandi through which criticism can be absorbed or deflected. In the note-sessions after rehearsals, his performance is finitely assessed by the director in terms which may be either positive or negative; encouraging or discouraging;   inspiring or humiliating. The graph of the actor's progress is open and public; so are the criticisms which track it from beginning to end.

Every actor adapts to criticism in ways personal to him or herself. Some actors feed on it masochistically - never happier than when they are being whipped towards higher and more unattainable results. Others resent it deeply, often tacitly, proffering an ostensible acceptance of it which disguises the resentment they are secretly harboring. The more rational artists weigh the director's findings with their own, assimilating certain points and rejecting others. The actors who openly acknowledge that they are merely accommodating-technicians assimilate everything they are told and shape their performance accordingly. The internal dialogue going on during a play-rehearsal is incessant. The director's voice, whether he realizes it or not, is only one of many voices echoing in the actor's head. It competes with the actor's own perceptions, the opinions of his fellow-players and that 'inner voice' which filters and modulates the flurry of impressions coming from all sources. It is busily decoding messages from the author, friends, 'significant others' and critics, dead or alive. The director, if he is forceful and has actually concocted an interpretation (as opposed to faking one as he goes along) is probably the most dominant influence for, in shaping the physical world of the play - the set, the blocking, the props and costumes - he is already inclining the actors towards his original intentions whether they acknolwedge it or not. The determining factor in any production is the physical milieu of a play and since traditionally, the director is responsible for that, he exerts an enormous influence on what actors do simply by establishing their context.

But behind all the doubts and uncertainties, the nagging questions and the endless changes, the actor is looking for affirmation, for certitude and unconsciously, for love. Making the right choice and then executing it well is a validation of both his skill and his taste and, until the play encounters its public, it is only the director who can confer that. Actors are not children nor is the director a paterfamilias, but the subconscious situation of play-production is that certain persons are 'at play' and one particular person is supervising that play, and the vestigial memories of childhood cannot help but affect such a situation, nor can the infantile urge for commendation and approval which childhood has lodged in our psyches. When, as children, we received the love and affection of our parents, it was gratutious. It came about because, in most cases, our parents loved us and wanted us to grow and develop, feel secure and wanted. Although the childhood paradigm is reinvoked in play-production, its purpose is very different. We 'play' in order to realize the meanings of our characters' lives and the fictional circumstances in which the playwrights have cast them. Our 'play' has clearcut objectives, and if they are not clear-cut, we constantly employ trial and error to divine them. Our play is predicated on organization rather than heedless spontaneity (although paradoxically, we attempt through organization to reproduce that spontaneity). And yet one similarity remains as deeply-rooted in us as when we were children: the need for approval from an authority-figure.

Can it be entirely expunged from acting? I doubt it. Should it be placed into a perspective appropriate to its professional aims and purposes? It must be - otherwise, while we are reexperiencing the fantasies of childhood, we may never know the gratifications of art.

*   *   *   *

THE NOTE SESSION

"Thank you for this final runthrough and excuse me for not dealing specifically with your performance, but tonight I felt it might be more useful if I made some general comments on what I've been feeling over the past few weeks since rehearsals began, as I've now become rather familiar with your strengths and weaknesses and the play will shortly open to the public.

"You know, the great pitfall of rehearsals is the natural tendency of actors to lose themselves either in their own roles or the contemplation of same. The repetitions that characterize rehearsals, the drilling of lines and moves, engender a kind of mesmerism in the actor and, although we are continually paying lip-service to contact, the absorption-with-self can sometimes become total. Quite understandably, here in the fourth week, your self-absorption is greater than it was in the first week when you were all trying to find your feet and work out your actions.

"By now most of you have sculpted your moments, gauged your effects and worked out a precise logic for what you are doing. Naturally, at this stage of the game, you need to solidify your performance so that it becomes almost involuntary - so you can push the start-button and just let it unwind - which of course, is not the same as as switching to automatic pilot - as nothing in acting can be 'automatic' if it's also going to be organic.

"Despite all our preparations, our organization of tempi and pace, we still do not know precisely to what degree we will convey our moments or project our characters. Only contact with the audience will determine that and, of course, it will change with each performance. All we can say with any degree of certainty is that we will probably do too much - give more than we should - for in performance, actors suddenly fall under the sway of what you might call, the Narrative-Imperative: succumbing to the temptation to dot every 'i' and cross every 't' to insure that every member of the audience fully understands the points we are intending to make.

"I would ask you to resist that inevitable temptation because it originates not in the soul of your character, but in the mushiness of your insecurity. The wish to inform with as much conciseness as possible is a journalistic temptation and not an artistic one. We must rely on our subtleties, our undercurrents, our innunedoes in order to convey dramatic information. Acting produces a kind of osmosis through which thoughts and feelings are silently transferred - received by the audience's transmittors through implication and indirection. If you take from the audience its god-given right to interpret your behavior and place on it what constructions it chooses, you violate the etiquette of the theatre; the unwritten rule which says that art infers and never declares, implies and never proclaims. You violate the audience's right to participate in the creative process and - although they never articulate it to themselves in quite that way - they will feel cheated and turn against you.

"The key to lightness in performance is 'touch and go' - make your point, do not malinger either to emphasize or indulge yourself, but go immediately to the next. Nothing in life stops to explain itself or reiterate its purpose. Things happen, move on to the next thing and change, either radically or infinitesimally, because of life's continuum. It is only bad art which malingers in order to reiterate, squeeze out its meaning, make sure its point has been taken.

"As I would warn you against the Narrative-Imperative, so I would ask you to guard against the Double-Glaze; that congealed state of emotional expression which tends to make you act *off* your partners rather than with them. We have all seen this glaze at one time or another. It is like a frozen blancmange on the actor's face signalling dramatic information while their true focus is concentrated in the auditorium. It is absence-of-mind engendered by the presence of the public. It is, to use a billiard term, like 'englishing' feelings off your partner so that they will sidle into the audience's pocket. A clear pane of glass enables you to see out and others to see in; double-glazing locks out sound and makes the object that bit more remote.

"For the past few weeks, you have been sharing rhythms with your fellow-actors. Together you have constructed a pattern of give-and-take which is now virtually fixed. But in a little while, a new factor will intrude into that pattern: the rhythm of the audience, and that will require you to open or close the pattern of your rhythm; to assimilate or block responses depending on whether they are useful or obstructive to the design you have already worked out. I don't simply mean that on occasion they may laugh and so your tempo must momentarily suspend to accomodate that laugh, I also mean that the rhythm-of-perception with which they receive the play's information has to be regulated according to your sense of what the audience is taking in, blocking or not understanding. That is done by a subtle adaptation of your breathing to theirs; by adjusting to the changing tempi by which they are assimilating your intentions. But the great danger here is that your carefully wrought rhythmic pattern may be disrupted due to eccentric or unpredictible reactions from different parts of the house. The audience is there to have the tempo of the performance imposed upon them. But their collective reactions entitle them to alter that tempo - to hasten or retard it - still, it remains the actors' responsibility to confer it. For in doing so, you are conferring the coagulated result of the entire rehearsal-period and that collective rhythm is as important as the shape and feel of any individual performance. Though it needs to be imposed, it mustn't be imposed arbitrarily. The company needs to adjust to the rhythm of the audience as if they were adapting to the arrival of a new character on stage - which in a sense, they are.

"Another thing. The public's arrival into the theatre brings with it an intense pressure. The worst aspect of this pressure is that it tends to dissolve the contact between player and player which many weeks of rehearsal have built up. The hardest thing in the world is, under the stress of public performance, to retain the network of private associations arduously crafted during rehearsals. It is pointless to exclaim "Concentrate, concentrate!' when everything happening on an opening-night conspires to throw your concentration into disarray. Therefore it is sometimes necessary to build a communal bulwark against the audience; to create, through group-exercises, a reaffirmation of the company's artistic identity.

"We will be doing vocal warm-ups and a certain amount of limbering before we step on stage, but more important than work on the voice or body is the tactile contact of one player with another. A collective physical embrace, corny as it may sound, is a way of experiencing the group-energy which will be necessarily partitioned on stage. It is also a way of reminding oneself of the make-up and character of the company which set out together many weeks ago and is now coming together to resolve the work it began. We hug each other when we part or when we reunite because, in the first instance, we want something of our bodily presence to be taken away, and in the second, because we want to reemphasize the closeness that existed before we parted. A collective physical embrace also reconfirms the unity of the joint effort; that although disparate, each with their respective roles and different personalities, we are still part of the same whole. If the rehearsal-period has not created the interconnecting vertabrae on which all ensemble depends, no amount of hugging is going to supply it. But if it has, the collective embrace is a kinetic reminder that each person in the production is in some way contingent upon the other.

"No doubt, as you play before the public, you will 'find things'. If the rehearsals are the runway, the performance is the lift-off and the weather-conditions you encounter up there, although predictable to some degree, are never precisely what you anticipated. That sense of discovery that comes through the presence of the public is the reason we have spent so much time preparing. It behooves us then to be as alert to the unexpected, as we are to the prearranged. Every performance, no matter how rigid the mise-en-scene, has an inescapable dimension of improvisation. The unforseen lurks behind every sculpted beat and the actor who can assimilate the New while conveying the Familiar is playing at peak efficiency. The worst thing is to assume that the production is a kind of music-box which, having been wound up, will automatically play the prescibed tune. That inclines actors into repeating last night's performance, or last week's, or even last month's, whereas the marvel of the theatre is that each night the play asks to be reborn. That can only happen if the actor is fertile; flexible, not fixed; open, not closed. Of course, the essence of what has been rehearsed is what has to be delivered, but there is always that extra dimension with a new house which makes each performance different from another.

"Finally, I want to say a word about 'notes.'

"There are three kinds of director's notes. The first exist in order to keep actors tied to the director's original blueprint, and night after night as they veer away from it, the director will try to draw them back to what was originally set. The second kind are there to monitor the inevitable changes that come about as a result of successive performances. These note-sessions acknowledge the fact that a role is something that lives and breathes within general parameters rather than a piece of human carpentry reducible to measurable millimetres. It assumes the actor will go a little too far in one direction or another, and should since, from night to night, audiences differ and so does the metabolism of each performance.

"The third kind of director's-notes assume that the premiere represents the cutting of the umbilical cord and that it is now up to the actor to develop his performance within the compass of the work achieved. The directors who follow that principle rarely visit the production after the opening - unless there are distressing reports of negligence or reversal. They are like the parents who cut the apron-strings and let their offsprings fend for themselves, reappearing only when they get into serious trouble.

"Let me tell you that I personally belong to the third category and so, if you see me again during the run of this play, it will be only to re-hearse understudies, incorporate rewrites or because some heinous sub-version has been committed which requires a stiff reprimand. Therefore, and I'm sure most of you will silently applaud this fact, I shall shortly be leaving you to your own devices. All the signals have been given, all the strategies prepared, now it is up to you to run with the play."

"Hamlet", Theatre of Cruelty Season at LAMDA

Phtograph by Michael Hardy

APHORISMS FOR THE YOUNG (AND NOT SO YOUNG) ACTOR

•A bad actor is someone who believes that speaking verse means no longer speaking English.

•Perversity is the name we give to objectionable originality.

•Creating a role before rehearsals commence is like preparing a meal in June which you intend to eat in December.

•If the opening-night is the birth of the performance, doesn't it stand to reason that by the closing-night it should have grown into something else?

•An actor who is himself lacking in character will always diminish the characters he is playing. An interesting actor is a gas-pump; a dull actor, a siphon.

•Inspiration is what happens when you temporarily loosen the grip on all your most firmly-held convictions.

•The most infectious disease in the theatre is boredom. No sooner does the actor feel it than it spreads to everyone else.

•If Shakespeare were alive today, he'd probably make a bee-line to the female mud-wrestling.

•In rehearsals, the discovery of a contradiction in one's role is like realizing in mid-flight that you've boarded the wrong plane.

•Actors spend a good part of their lives analyzing the greatest works of dramatic literature. They probe the deepest motives of their characters and try to correlate them to the themes of the plays they are performing. In researching their work, they study different periods of history, manners, customs and philosophies. They delve into psychology and search for motivation. They dissect language and discriminate between what ancient words used to mean and what they mean today. They probe text, challenge directors and are avid readers of criticism but, as a group, are invariably considered to be non-intellectual. - Compared to most brokers, salesmen, attorneys, accountants, journalists, publicists, tradesmen, soldiers, politicians, or clerics, they are mental giants.

•Assigning an actor to a vocal coach in the middle of a production is like applying a band-aid to a broken leg.

•An actor who burrows so deeply into his role that he severs contact with his fellow-players is like a man digging his own grave in the mistaken belief that he is prospecting for gold.

•The worst insult to an actor is being left to his own devices after a director has tried and failed to achieve a desired result.

•If, while the actors are performing, the public hears only the playwright's voice, the theatre is being abused. If, after the performance, the public recalls only the actor's voice and not the playwright's, a like offense has been committed.

•The actor who prides himself on being instinctive rather than intellectual is like a man who claims that since he has eyes he doesn't need ears.

•There is nothing more antipathetic to art than an actor constantly wanting to be 'sympathetic' to his audience. In almost every case, it is a symptom of a woeful failing in the actor's character. The only thing more repugnant than playing for laughs is playing for love.

•The most bloodcurdling moment in the theatre is produced when an actor looks into another actor's eyes and sees there only the terror of forgetfulness.

•Historically speaking, the avant-garde was a turn of the century phenomenon. To be labeled 'avant garde' today usually means the work in question is about a hundred years out of date.

•The mark of a strong actor is his desire to be surrounded by people better than himself. The mark of a weak actor, the paranoia occasioned by precisely the same thing.

•The actor who leaves rehearsals without at least one idea more than when he arrived ought to volunteer to have his salary docked.

•I've got a System said the Russian. I've got Theory said the German. I've got a Method said the American. I've got a distinct pain in the butt, says the public.

•An insatiable desire for stardom is often the creative artist's most effective fuel. Desperately wanting to be famous often unlocks creative reserves that are shut tight to people who are indifferent to career.

•The actor wants love. The director wants power. The playwright wants fame. The public wants twenty minutes off the second act. Nobody gets what they want.

•A director returning to a play after it has opened and launched its run is like a man trying to revive a love affair with a mistress who has since married and had twelve chldren.

•Nothing is but interpretation makes it so.

•I rethink therefore I am.

•For a director, relinquishing a fallacious idea is like losing a limb. For an actor, it's like sprouting wings,

•The best way to escape the tyranny of the clock is to fill up the minutes and ignore the hours.

•There are three people who should be summarily executed in the theatre: 1) the stage-manager who, slave to the clock, ends a rehearsal when an actor is in the full flush of creation, 2) the actor who in order to 'save himself' for the performance plays run-throughs at half-cock and 3) the director who believes that the best way to deal with a bad actor is to fill him with false confidence.

•An actor who cannot bear the sting of a director's criticisms will have to bear the bludgeon of an audience's rejection.

•A bad costume-designer uses an actor as a mannequin; a good one, as a canvas.

•Sometimes there is more animosity in a dressing-room than is to be found in the collected works of Marlowe, Webster, Strindberg, Mamet or John Osborne. A warm-up in hell never leads to a heavenly performance.

•The face of the actor who vigorously nods his agreement to a director's criticism but tacitly rejects it, never throws back a reflection in a dressing-room mirror.

•A rehearsal that doesn't begin in the boiler-room will never make it to the penthouse.

•The hardest thing for a director ever to get out of an actor is the right inflection. An inflection is the expression of a subtlety-of-thought and an actor incapable of having that thought can never articulate it convincingly. That is why explaining the meaning of a line is always preferable to demonstrating how it should be read.

•A set design that looks complete without a single actor in front of it is usually flawed in some subtle but fundamental way.

•In life, we never dissociate feeling from language. We feel, we speak. Only in the theatre, do we first learn the words, and then add the feelings. Like painting by numbers.

•Often, the only consolation of an actor who is thoroughly disliked by all his fellow-actors is that he is beloved by the public.

•Just as the child is totally oblivious of the doctor who has delivered him, the actor after an opening-night cannot believe he didn't emerge into the world entirely on his own volition.

•A dramaturg is a pimp who takes a fee from both the whore and the john.

•A photo-call attended by members of the press represents an incursion of ends into means. It brings hard, cold, careerist thoughts into a realm which, for weeks, has been carefully sealed off from such considerations. It reminds actors that there will be a public reckoning for all the private work in which they have been engaged. The best way to handle a photo-call is not to have one.

•The actor who gets buoyed up by the enthusiasm of a moronic audience is like an addict getting his kicks from placebos.

•The last refuge of an actor imprisoned in a hopeless turkey which has been demolished by all the critics, is always: "The *audience* enjoyed it."

•The best way to gauge the effect of a play is the morning after. If its memory hasn't made it through the night, it's probably nothing to write home about.

•The actor's unshakable conviction that he is embroiled in the worst piece of crap ever assembled on any stage can be instantaneously banished by one insincere compliment.

•The successful actor of contemporary plays who is afraid to tackle Shakespeare is the equivalent of the dieter who claims to have lost twenty pounds but refuses to step on a scale to prove it.

•There is a kind of director who is essentially the chairman of a committee. He allows each member to have his say, takes sides with no one and makes sure that everyone casts his vote. He is useless as as director, but companies always adore him.

•The best way to exacerbate an acting-problem is for a director who cannot put his finger on its cause to bring it to the actor's attention.

•The difficulties created by a 'difficult actor' are usually what makes the theatre soar. The genial, easygoing actors with whom no one ever has any trouble are the ciphers of the profession.

•A placid rehearsal period overflowing with bonhomie and free of conflict is invariably a harbinger of failure.

•An actress highly susceptible to tears is usually crying about things that have everything to do with her life and nothing to do with her role.

•Arbitrarily imposing a period-style on a Shakespearean play without justifying the parallels is like being naked underneath a large raccoon coat.

•No matter how accomplished the prose-actor may be, he will be unbearable when he turns verse into prose.

•If it takes approximately four weeks for an actor to figure out a character's nature and psychology, how can a designer decide what clothes he should be wearing months in advance?

•Only the actor who masters the intricacies of the verse has a chance of realizing the poetry.

•The rehearsal-period does not give birth to the production; it merely fertilizes the ovum with sperm. Birth, if one is lucky, is what happens between the opening and the closing.

•If the rational mind is percipient enough to discern "the irrational," should we not believe that, at some point, all irrationality will be capable of explication?

•Everyone's reality is different. A diskette that cannot be read by one computer is perfectly readable on another. When we dismiss something because it doesn't make sense, are we not simply saying *we* cannot make sense of it. If it is 'readable' on other people's logic-board is that not a criticism of our own hardwiring?

•Harold Clurman used to say he never came across any play which wasn't 'realistic' - i.e. that didn't in some way or other derive from reality. I think he meant that anything that came from the mind of man, no matter how abstruse, had to have some bearing on mankind. Does that entirely abolish genres such as Surrealism, Expressionism or the Absurd? No, it merely emphasizes the necessity to delineate the subtle differences that exist between styles.

•The greatest narrative-making machine in the world is our dream-life. The capacity to dream, which belongs to literally everyone, is what makes artists out of all of us. There is no one, no matter how dull and untalented, who doesn't produce rich dramatic constructions during sleep. Art is the language which enables us to inter-communicate on the level of dreams. If we didn't all have suspended animation in common, we could never suspend our disbelief in the theatre. 'Suspending our disbelief' is just another way of saying we are capable of collective dreaming. In that regard, art and life are not separate, but one.

•There is an assumption in the theatre that because something happens on a stage which no one has ever seen before, an artistic innovation has taken place. But calamities, novelties, eccentricities and examples of appalling bad taste fall just as readily into that category.

•Art which isn't fun isn't art.

"Hamlet", Theatre of Cruelty Season at LAMDA

Phtograph by Michael Hardy

*　　*　　*　　*　　*　　*

THE NEW ACTING

Naturalism, as it took shape in the late 19th century, was an attempt to recreate the externals of truthful behavior. Based on science and fastidious historical accuracy, it tried to replace the fustian and bombast of romantic acting styles with studiously organized verisimilitude. Suspicious of art, it drew all its models from what was observable in Nature.

Realism, also prompted by scientific discoveries (particularly in psychology) went one step further, trying not only to hold the mirror up to nature but making it concave so that it would also reflect internal states. By the time the 20th century got into its stride, Expressionism and Dada made that liberating leap beyond verismo into dreams and fantasy and from there, it was a short step to Surrealism, Theater of the Absurd, Antonin Artaud, Jean Genet and Samuel Beckett.

From the 1920s onward, almost every advance in theatrical style was justified both as a flight from realism and an advance towards greater truth. The avowed tendency was to discard art (i.e. traditional constructs) and confront life directly. What Brecht, Meyerhold, Artaud, Grotowski, Brook, Kantor and The Living Theatre all had in common was the desire to abandon rigid performance conventions so as to be able to deal more freely (i.e. more truthfully) with reality; to penetrate, as Artaud described it, "that fragile, fluctuating center which forms never reach."

At the root of all the theories promulgated by these theatre-artists was the assumption, stated or implied, that the driving force behind the experimental new techniques was a more accurate interpretation of human experience. 'Telling it how it is' as opposed to how theatrical conventions obliged it to be falsified because of the atrophy of their forms. In a sense, it was more a philosophic than an esthetic quest. One could not deal, for instance, with Beckett without addressing questions of Being and Nothingness or Ionesco without entering into a critique of language. Interpreting the plays of Jean Genet obliged critics to elucidate questions of ontology and sexual fantasy. One could not speak of Bertolt Brecht without noting his ideological debt to Hegel and Marx. The Surrealists were profoundly inspired by the precepts of Sigmund Freud. The dramatists had become the philosophers and to properly interpret the motions of the new drama necessitated reference to categories-of-thought such as Existentialism, Semantics, Metaphysics, Dialectical Materialism and Psychoanalysis.

What precisely, is the difference between Life and Art?

Life is flux, unvariegated, aimless, disorderly, discontinuous and non-sequential. Art, even in its most anarchic and revolutionary forms, involves order, assembly, structure and intention - even when the intention is anti-art. But over the years, it is precisely this 'ordering' of life through art which has falsified it; made it pat and simplistic; formulaic and unconvincing. The surge towards Expressionism then

Surrealism then the Absurd to what we now woolily call post-modernism, has been a series of attempts to counter the limitations of preceding forms - to grapple with that streaming, intangible, ineluctable flow which we recognize as the source of art but disparage for its partiality and lack of depth.

It is this fierce dissatisfaction with the conventions developed since the beginning of the century which has impelled artists to abandon form altogether and make a charge at essence itself. They have tried to express and interpret life by diving full force into its labyrinth. Hence, the recent spate of One Man and One Woman Shows (often cited as examples of 'performance art' but essentially, unwinnowed monologues) in which individual subjectivities are excavated and then put on display in a confessional style reminiscent of the analysand. Hence the abandonment of traditional means such as narrative, sequential development, logical continuity and linear form. Hence the adoption of techniques, mannerisms and innovations whose appeal lies mainly in the fact that they do not duplicate or resemble the work of previous artists or established modes of expression.

But in sidestepping established conventions and short-circuiting the art-life equation on which traditional art has been based, the artist has paradoxically returned to his starting-point. No longer armed with tools with which to hack order out of chaos, he stands helplessly before the chaos, mirroring it, becoming one with it. Being part of the flux, he no longer sees it in perspective. The fundamental standoffishness which gives the artist the objectivity with which to make something meaningful of his subjective experience has been abandoned in favor of 'the thing itself' - overlooking the fact that 'the thing itself,' shorn of

measurable parameters and communicable forms is intrinsically meaningless.

Both life and art contain ceremonies, rituals, actions, paradoxes,
contradictions, ideas and feelings which ask to be both reconciled and
kept separate. The function of art is to shape these things, the purpose
of life merely to experience them. By eradicating the line that separates
life and art, the artist relinquishes the right to deal with esthetics at all
for, in order to express value-judgments about the flux, reflection is essential and that is precisely what being enmeshed in life militates
against.

The tendency to push beyond the doctrines of art leads the artist
not to the fringes of 'the cutting-edge' but into that unvariegated
wilderness which inspired his desire to discriminate between life and
art in the first place. Push a radical to his logical extreme, they say, and
he becomes a reactionary. Push the methodology of art to its furthest
extreme and you are left with the morass out of which the very first
artist attempted to bring order out of chaos. The artist who out of exasperation with the limitations of his art-form turns to the public for direct communion is like the priest who abandons his ministry to wallow
in the very venality he is being asked to absolve. It is a merging of functions which, in order to be efficacious, need to be separated.

Julian Beck whose productions with The Living Theatre were in
many ways the most extreme (and most successful) version of this anti-
art attitude has written:

"We said in preparing 'Paradise Now' that we wanted to make a play which would no longer be enactment but would be the act itself; that we should not reproduce something but we would try to create an event in which we would always ourselves be experiencing it, not anew at all but something else each time; not reproducing and bringing to life the same thing again and again and again, but always it would be a new experience for us and it would be different from what we called acting."

Behind this wish is the artist's understandable exasperation with art's inadequacy to deal directly with the flux. Instead of shaping it, giving it finite structure, accountable point and purpose, Beck, says: "Let us assault it on its own terms; let us meld with it and accept every manifestation of our action, and the audience's, as part of whatever organic process exists. Let us be one with the Life Force!"

"Of all your works," I wrote to the Becks in a review in <u>The New York Times</u>, "I think *Paradise Now* has gone furthest in obliterating that impregnable line that separates life and art. By asserting that whatever happens on the evening is part of the event, you have created a marvelously open-ended structure which clearly defies critical analysis. As with all happenings, the judgment of the evening is a judgment on oneself. One gets from it what one is prepared to bring."

Which is perhaps a fanciful way of saying that like all improvisationally-geared public events, it is brought down to its lowest common denominator. Being essentially a provocation rather than a declaration, it incites indiscriminate crowd-reactions and expressions of mob-hysteria rather than considered thought, and reduces issues to shibboleths. (The 'issues' themselves in 'Paradise Now' were rather primitive to start with: passport abolition, repeal of drug-legislation, the sanctioning of nudity, an appeal to universal commonality as opposed to hierar-chical social-structure, etc.). Within the catch-all framework of such a 'show', the artists could only express jargon and the audience could only respond either with heckles or huzzahs. It wasn't the content of "Paradise Now" which made it excitable and memorable, it was the form - but contrary to the truism, the form was not inextricable from the content. Each could be distinctively discerned, the one having been consciously molded onto the other.

The performance took the form of a collective assault, using con-trasting segments vaguely allied to radical or anti-authoritarian atti-tudes-of-mind, deftly assimilating audience reaction as it occurred and stuffing the esthetic distance that traditionally exists between actors and audience with a variety of vocal and kinetic tactics designed to jostle awareness on specific social and political subjects. The show, despite its intellectual pretensions, was almost all physicality - but the latter did not edify, illustrate or persuade in regard to the former. In its vibrant heart and woolly head, it merely dispensed 60's-honed banalities.

But it did generate an unmistakable excitement derived largely from that sense of danger which ensues when wild animals are reported to have escaped their cages and are roaming free in the neighborhoods. That is a palpable sensation and I do not mean to belittle its dramatic effect by comparing actors to wild animals; the creation of that kind of tension within the framework of a theatrical entertainment is a real achievement and should not be sold short. No well-coordinated, com-fortably-subsidized, thoroughly-sanitized repertory company or re-gional theatre could have produced "Paradise Now" and no company locked into conventional morality could have conceived it.

But we are concerned here with the texture and import of performance; what it is that happens when actors abdicate their traditional responsibilities - characterization, story-telling, mounting tension, denouement, etc - and fling their naked and unadorned selves at a public with whom they assume an inextricable commonality.

There is a dynamic import in the very act of pulling down convention - similar to that produced when an obsolete tower-block is dynamited to make way for a new construction. The catharsis achieved by throwing traditional catharses to the wind is considerable and since we are dealing with an art-form that is constantly trying to intensify its effect on the public, we have to acknowledge the pure dramatic value to be gained from tactics which renounce or transcend conventional stage practices.

Having acknowledged that, we have to go on to assess the intrinsic, that's to say, durable value of such a performance, since we all know there are certain moral and sexual buttons we can push in order to disturb an audience or provoke it to outrage. We expect something more lasting from art and, although the past provides us with examples of great art which have defined themselves by outraging the public, we have learned since the advent of modernism to be wary of works which do only that. Jarry incensing a bourgeois Parisian public in 1896 or Stravinsky doing the same in 1912 is not the same thing as a self-styled 'enfant terrible' deliberately setting out to catch tomorrow's headlines with calculated demonstrations of novelty and nudity. In a sense, artists such as Jarry, Picasso and Stravinsky have made it impossible for contemporary artists to reproduce the avant garde audacity of the past. Those genuine breakthroughs have obliged modern artists to find very different ways in which to 'epater le bourgeois' - given the fact that the bourgeosie has completely changed its social make-up and are much less vulnerable to shock than their ancestors of eighty and a hundred years ago. When avant-garde art becomes nostalgic, it tends to mindlessly replicate the effects of its pioneers of a century ago and, paradoxically, becomes reactionary.

But in the Happenings of the 60s, the performance-art of the 80s and 90s and certain outré productions of groups such as Mabou Mines and the Wooster Group, acting has deliberately couched itself in stark, kinetic, non-naturalistic terms, aiming for effects very far removed from empathy or verisimilitude. Stanislavsky and Brecht are of no use in training actors for such work because psychological plausibility and political suasion do not figure prominently in its intentions. Here, the actor is a kind of objective unit in a visual-auditory-and-kinetic masterplan whose larger aim is a multi-media assault on the audience's sensibilities and the projection of broad, bold imagery. But free-form though it may be, 'acting' is still going on and the energy, attack and communicative skills we traditionally associate with the art, are still at play.

The 'actor' in such spectacles (and often non - actors are preferred) has to assimilate the style of the piece much more assiduously than in conventional drama. A Robert Wilson version of "King Lear" for instance, demands an objectivity of performance very different from that required by a conventional rendering of Shakespeare's play. Literally used as an object, the actor has to perform within a strict metrical framework, counting rather than experiencing his beats, often assuming an anonymity which is the very opposite of delineated characterization. The goal is no longer to create emotion by engendering it oneself and then radiating it outward to one's public, but executing a variety of physical chores which, in the assembled context, will produce an ambiguous effect. It is a form of acting which denies that most treasured of all the actor's means: subjectivity - emphasizing instead his presence as a visible, tangible essentially 'cool' factor in a mise-en-scene, the quintessence of what Brecht tried and failed to achieve in his own work: a state of objectivity free of tanked-up emotions and devoted to a larger intellectual design which, objectively structured is also objectively perceived.

In solo performance art, which proliferated in the mid and late 80s and still flourishes today, the 'actor,' unlike traditional One Man and Woman shows based on the biographical recreation of historical personalities, is projecting his or her own sensibility often with the aid of highly-personalized material. Traditional monologists (i.e. Will Rogers, George Jessel, Ruth Draper) disseminated aperçus through their own personality but in the main, concealed themselves behind their material; i.e projected a stage-persona through which their observations could be conveyed. Performance-artists such as John Fleck, Tim Miller, Karen Finley, and Spalding Gray posit their own views in their own personalities; the core of their subjectivity is part-and-parcel of their art. Although there is still structure and format, the thrust of their performances is contained more in who they are than in what they are saying; indeed; who they are entirely conditions what they are saying and there is no effort made to separate the two.

Here one is acting ones' self in a way never intended by Stanislavsky who always assumed the role was the mask through which the soul of the actor would reveal itself. Here, the actor is obliged to project reminiscence, insight, philosophy and anecdote with the same directness of communication that might apply in a non-theatrical setting. He is, in a very real sense, acting his being, and although it may appear to be effortless, it requires an extraordinary effort to project, in artificial surroundings, what appears to be one's natural persona; the former having an irresistible tendency to falsify the latter. To preserve his naturalness in the artificial context, an actor like Spalding Gray places rivets of fixed gestures into his monologues and posits specific bits of business which, like so many tent-pins, support the canopy of his material. Performance artists such as Tim Miller and John Fleck move from one visual image to the other, allowing the flow of language to rise and dip according to the stations through which it passes. The assumption behind many of these monologues is that the performer is addressing the audience and deliberately denying esthetic distance. The theatre becomes a room; the actor, a conversationalist; the public, a confidante. What 'art' there may be is deliberately ground into an atmosphere of informality.

In full-scale performance art pieces, the tendency is to curb 'acting' so that it resists conventional theatricality and functions merely as part of a larger whole. This is why, perhaps, traditionally-trained actors shun such works. For many of them, it is the denial of what acting is supposed to be: viz. broad, energized, ostentatious, personalized. But since Brecht, there has been a tendency in the theatre to turn the actor into something other than the bold, palpitating, rhetorical creature he has become and, curiously, in Performance Art, that tendency has been taken to its logical conclusion. The actor is asked to function as part - and by no means the most prominent part - of a larger whole and when he is effectively subordinated into the mesh, as is often the case with the work of Robert Wilson and Richard Foreman, he acquires a formal identity.

Performance Art brought forth the proposition that everything was possible in art and that art and technology, those two sworn enemies, could not only share the same bed but happily copulate between the sheets. As a result, every artist no matter what his or her discipline, has had to adjust to a new esthetic dispensation, one in which some of their traditional turf has had to be sacrificed in return for new and unanticipated gains in other areas. The composer has lost his autonomy, but gained exciting new collaborators. The painter has been forced out of his gallery but acquired a much larger canvas. The actor has lost some of his simulations but gained an existentialist dimension not previously available to him. His domain has been expanded beyond the playhouse, beyond the scope of his personal creativity, beyond the realm of any single playwright's limited imagination. He literally has been freed and, with his newfound freedom, has been obliged to cultivate new skills, new work-methods and a new relationship to the public. Acting has burst the bounds into which theorists like Delsarte and Diderot would have imprisoned it. Having started by blurring the line between life and art, it has now erased it altogether.

And yet we still speak about the actor as if he were a person who simply donned a costume and applied make-up and we still train him as if physical deportment and vocal technique were his two main attributes. Even as we acknowledge the new parameters of his calling, we exhort him to revere the old-fashioned traditions from which the 20th century has dramatically released him. It is because this paradox exists between what he was and what he has now become that we are obliged to redefine his function and rethink his training, and it is precisely because his profession refuses to recognize these new acquisitions that the new actor must recognize them for himself.

Whether a marriage will ever take place between the esthetics of Performance Art and traditional theatre remains to be seen. At the moment, there is something tantalizing about an artistic off-shoot that utilizes all the ingredients of theatre and at the same time spurns its traditional aims. By giving parity to sound, movement, design and music, Performance Art, at its best, provides more stimuli than is usually attainable from conventional playgoing. In by-passing or subordinating language, it prevents the art-form from merely duplicating the effects of television or cinema. It more easily integrates the latest electronic advances - i.e. lasers, computerized design, digital sound-techniques - and thereby seems more at home with the technological vocabulary which conventional theatre-practice has not yet assimilated. How the actor must adapt himself to these changes is a question not yet addressed by theatre schools or academies and it is because the actor's traditional work seems so alien to the new form that its practitioners tend to shy away from using 'professionals.' But if the actor can be persuaded that 'acting' need not, in every case, involve the construction of three-dimensional characters within a realistic framework or be circumscribed by boundaries drawn by the playwright or dictated by the director, Performance Art offers a fertile field for genuine artistic expansion.

Just as the anti-theatre experiments of playwrights such as Jarry, Arrabal, Ionesco, Genet, Beckett, Peter Handke and Botho Straus gave fascinating new wrinkles to traditional theatre writing, so, paradoxically, the tendency towards anti-acting promises to enrich the art of the actor. There never is a birth of a new form without the placenta of the old still clinging to its body, but once the umbilical cord is cut, the possibilities are endless.

*   *   *   *

THE CLASSICAL STRETCH

You've got that suicidal look in your eyes again. What's the problem today?

After having played a whole range of realistic roles in contemporary plays, I find myself a little daunted by Shakespeare. I mean, I understand what's going on; I understand the 'actions' and 'objectives' of characters like Richard III, for instance, the sub-text of his scenes, the feelings he is expressing, but I don't seem to be able to get these things across.

You mentioned the "actions and objectives," the "sub-text" and "feelings," but what about the language?

Well of course, I understand the language; I mean, there are certain archaic words that I had to look up but, by and large, I understand what the characters are saying.

What about the verse?

Well, it's iambic pentameter isn't it: five beats to the line and the stress on the second syllable.

You mean on every second syllable?

The iamb means one short syllable followed by a long syllable, right?

Well, let's see:

> Now 'is the 'win-ter 'of our 'dis-con'tent
> Made 'glor-ious 'Summer 'by this 'Son of 'York
> And 'all the 'clouds that 'lowere'd u'pon our 'house
> In 'the deep `'bosom 'of the 'O-cean 'buried.

Like that?

Well no, not like that - that sounds singsong and stupid.

But it's a short foot followed by a long foot with a stress on the second syllable.

It still sounds stupid.

Right, so I guess you mean it's not necessary to stress every second syllable. So there are some words that need stress and others that don't. Some words that weigh heavier than others. What about that first line; what are the key words there, would you say?

"Now," I guess, and "winter" and "discontent?"

So assist-words like "is the" and "of our" kind of ride along while key words get stressed. And, as you indicated, it makes more sense to stress "Now" than "is" even though metrically, the stress belongs to "is." So the rule about scansion is pretty flexible; in fact, stress is determined not by rules of prosody but what you mean to say.

But I thought the point was to try to figure out what Shakespeare *meant to say.*

No one's been able to figure that out for over 400 years; I mean defin-
itively. We know, or think we know, what the lines mean and more or
less, what the plays are about, but every time we see an innovative revival, they seem to be about something else - so obviously, the works
are immensely mutable. And what enables them to 'mean' different
things from one generation to the next are the impressions they create
on their various interpreters. Although we can pretty well determine
the sense of the lines, the meaning of the plays are constantly transforming.

But there must be certain principles regarding the verse, mustn't there?

Principles, no. Guidelines, yes. For instance, we know that when we
observe the enjambment in lines like:

> "Since my dear soul was mistress of her choice
> And could of men distinguish, her election
> Hath sealed thee for herself. For thou hast been
> As one, in suff'ring all, that suffers nothing,
> A man that Fortune's buffets and rewards
> Has ta'en with equal thanks; and blest are those
> Whose blood and judgement are so well commin-
> gled
> That they are not a pipe for Fortune's finger
> To sound what stop she please. Give me that man
> That is not passion's slave, and I will wear him
> In my heart's core, ay, in my heart of heart,

As I do thee."

It makes sense to wrap the first three lines up to "sealed thee for herself" into one unit, and then to make one long run-on sentence of the next seven lines, ending with a coda on the last line beginning with "Give me that man...." Enjambment is a guideline for the sense, but it's not a principle as there are many speeches that contain enjambment which can be played without necessarily rolling on to succeeding lines.

Also, it is usually the case that when you have a series of short lines, all making up a foot of iambic pentameter, it is usually an indication that they should be played quickly to complete the measure. But even that 'rule' is not graven in stone and there are innumerable instances when the broken phrases, as in "Macbeth" for instance, instead of running together are divided by pauses and business:

LADY MACBETH   Did not you speak?

MACBETH: When?

LADY MACBETH: Now?

MACBETH: As I descended.

LADY MACBETH: Ay.

MACBETH: Hark!
Who lies i' the second chamber?

LADY MACBETH: Donalbain.

The only 'principle' that I can discern is that once the actor has determined his meaning and can make the text convey it, the rhythm of the verse has to adapt to whatever is necessary to make that meaning 'read' to an audience.

Even if it means getting away from scansion?

If you follow scansion slavishly, you can't help but produce a kind of doggerel. It's like strictly observing punctuation in contemporary prose. If you were to do that, you'd find yourself talking like a robot.

Sense determines rhythm, intention determines stress. The verse is clay not marble and it is the actor who operates the potter's wheel. Scansion is often a good guide as to which word should be emphasized over another, but you've always got a choice of between three to five words and it's up to you - your sense, that is - as to where the stress mainly should fall.

Somehow, I don't know why, I always feel phony reciting Shakespeare's lines. Like being someone I'm not.

That's a common feeling - especially for American actors. Clearly, the language is heightened English speech and often expresses heightened emotion. It's not the way we normally express ourselves, but it is often the poetic expression of many of the things we think and feel. The Doctor during Lady Macbeth's sleepwalking scene says:

> "Foul whisperings are abroad, unnatural deeds
> Do breed unnatural troubles; infected minds
> To their deaf pillows will discharge their secrets.

More needs she the divine than the physician."

We might paraphrase that as: "There's alot of nasty rumors circulating. Guilty people sometimes dream things they would never dare express in public. She'd be better off confessing her sins to a priest than seeking out a doctor." The sense of the speech is crystal-clear though the language is highly wrought, but there is nothing in the speech that can't be conveyed in a contemporary tone and which wouldn't make sense of the Doctor's troubled concern and the implications of what he has heard. In instances like that, we simply play the sense of Shakespeare's language. But when we have sentiments like Albany's at the end of KING LEAR:

> "The weight of this sad time we must obey:
> Speak what we feel, not what we ought to say.
> The oldest hath borne the most; we that are
>   young
> Shall never see so much nor live so long."

Shakespeare is loading language with almost more than it can bear. These are ideas that cannot be simply paraphrased without immense loss. The full brunt of Lear's agony is contained in those words - as well as a prophecy that future generations will suffer similar cruelties although the pain may not be as great. It is a quatrain full of grief as well as a kind of forlorn hope, and what makes it register with the audience is our memory of Lear's recent turmoils; the King's pathetic descent from sovereignty; his madness; the torture inflicted by Regan and Goneril; the murder of his beloved Cordelia.

In other words, it isn't the verse alone which is carrying the burden of the drama. The language is the accumulation of all the actions which have preceded it and that is what gives those words their intellectual resonance. Perhaps an average member of the audience would not be able to explain that final quatrain, but in an effective production of "Lear," he or she can't help being affected by it. It is almost the sound alone which triggers the catharsis; the sound plus the dire incidents which have been witnessed during the preceding three hours. There comes a point, in any great drama, where language, no matter how eloquent, simply loses effect. Events have already lodged themselves so deeply into the metabolism that it simply doesn't matter any longer what people say.

I keep getting stymied by the fact that no matter how strong my emotion, it doesn't seem to get through the language.

Feeling is the greatest pitfall in Shakespeare because feeling that blurs the imagery or saturates the words can dislocate the verse. We now understand that with Shakespeare, it is often a matter of working backward from language. Instead of going from the inside out, as the Method dictates, it's a matter of working from the outside in. Nor is this, as some people seem to believe, an external approach. The fact is it doesn't matter one whit if the relevant emotions are motivated from the language to the character or the other way around. In Shakespeare, it is often the case that the language graphically describes the emotion. "Now could I drink hot blood/And do such bitter business as the day/Would quake to look on," clearly expresses a vengeful surge in Hamlet's soul and needs no emotional overlay to make its point. When Gertrude says: "Thou turn'st mine eyes into my very soul/And there I see such black and grained spots/As will not leave their tinct," her words so perfectly encapsulate her guilt that to paint guilt on top of them is redundant. Of course, the speeches need to be tinted with the emotion they are expressing, but not submerged; otherwise the feeling diffuses the words and one gets neither the emotion nor the poetry.

Now wait a minute. According to what I've been taught, the point is to muster up the feeling indicated by the text - so that the actor can reach the point where the emotion justifies the words.

But in Shakespeare it often happens that the emotion is articulated through the words. In a modern play, a powerful moment may be one in which the actor is strangulated with emotion, made breathless or incoherent. In prose writing, nothing may be lost when such an emotion is conveyed; indeed, it may often be relevant for language to be either subordinated or even suspended. But in Shakespeare, the emotion is often inseparable from the verse which contains it, and so to lose the language is to muddy up the feeling. Besides, the greatest passion is often contained in the verbal imagery. What happens in badly-acted classics is that the audience is asked to accept a banal emotional reaction in place of the subtlety-of-feelings described in the text.

No, a description of a feeling is never the equivalent of a truly-felt and clearly expressed emotion, but in Shakespeare, the actor learns how to balance feeling and verse so that one is reinforcing the other. To assume that the veracity of an emotion is somehow superior to the language which poetically describes it is to entirely misunderstand the nature of blank verse and the conventions in which Shakespeare wrote.

Well what happens when an actor decides to interpret a classic in contemporary terms - that is, when the period is dropped and the interpretation is couched in a modern idiom; sometimes even played in modern dress? Then you've got contemporary characters speaking period verse but relaying a very different story from the one Shakespeare originally told.

So long as the language is retained, the traditional problems remain. You can, as John Hirsch did in his Iran-Contra adaptation of "Coriolanus," adopt a conversational rhythm and a prosaic approach to the verse, but you have to be prepared to sacrifice language for modernity. Sometimes, as in Hirsch's case, the swap makes sense and most of the time, the exciting physicality of the production was an acceptable substitute for the loss of language. But by and large, audiences feel cheated when the verse is jettisoned. After all, it is through the verse that the conflicts operate and the characters interact, so when you chuck that out, or seriously subordinate it, you are working against yourself.

However, it isn't an either-or situation. It is perfectly possible to let the language do its job while the panoply of the play is radically altered. It's just that for actors, a modern approach to a classic is often taken as an invitation to be sloppy and imprecise, casual and slipshod. The plays were conceived as formal structures and casual behavior and casual speech run against their grain. But it's worth noting that during Peter Hall's directorship of the Royal Shakespeare Company, one saw the Henry plays in 'The Wars of the Roses' played with unmistakable modern allusions, but still in period dress and in keeping with the plays' historicity. So it doesn't follow that to be 'modern' one has to resort to modern dress and haul in obvious topical allusions. In fact, the question could be put: how can contemporary actors playing to a contemporary audience conditioned by 20th century ideas be anything other than 'modern?' The greatness of the plays, it seems to me, is that they can be used to convey ideas very far removed from the ones that Shakespeare originally intended. Is this being unfaithful to the text? I think not. On the contrary, it is being faithful to the plays' essential mutability; their ability endlessly to permute with the passage of time.

What is *unfaithful* is trying to fix a classic in an earlier mold - to revive it according to the discoveries and insights of a previous generation and in a style that was once lauded but has now been superseded.

The thing is, I need a peg for a character like Richard III; I can't play an historical idea that I've only read about; that doesn't connect up with my own personal experience. That would be dry and academic. I need to base my Richard on someone specific like Stalin or Hitler, Mao or Ceasescue.

Virtually every performance an actor gives is based on an ur-character; that is, someone or other that they associate with the role they are playing; someone they can identify with. Most of the time, it's unconscious, but alot of the time, it's very specific. So long as the ur-character nourishes and conditions your character, there's a value in making that kind of correlation. But when the ur-character replaces the character - when Richard *becomes* Stalin or Sir Oswald Mosley (as was the case with Ian McKellan's 'Richard'), you get not so much a diminution of Shakespeare as a cloaking of the role's energy. Because you see, a character like Richard is not *only* political; he has a number of other dimensions which Shakespeare has provided and which tend to get shorn away as soon as the character gets masked - i.e. turned into an identifiable historical character. It's really a subtle kind of exploitation. Shakespeare is being used to convey values, ideas, attitudes and opinions which, though analogous to the play's content, are presented as if they were identical to it. The insights of the original work, which would have enabled an audience to draw their own connections to the historical counterparts, are taken from the audience and turned into editorial comment. The audience is cheated of subtlety and the artist exchanges ambiguity for explicitness.

But everyone agrees that the point of reviving Shakespeare's plays is for them

to have some contemporary relevance, and surely, drawing those kinds of par-
allels is a way of doing just that.

Exactly - it's a way of doing *'just'* that - but there is a great deal more to
be done with the work than using it as a transparency for a topical allusion. As soon as you impose a specific historical period (let's say the
1930s as McKellan did) and a set of recognizable characters (say, Wally
Simpson or Oswald Mosley), you are not only drawing resemblances,
you are also positing the values of the new period. The costumes, the
make-up, the settings, they all possess social connotations which can't
help being thrown into the mix. If your parallels are magically exact,
then that's fine. You've managed to take a period artifact and a clutch
of contemporary ideas and turn them into one indissoluble unit. But
the chances of effecting that kind of exact fit are rare, and when the elements don't quite marry, you have a number of contradictions in the
way that characters speak and behave, look and act. You can, as is the
case in most contemporary versions of Shakespeare, iron out the differences but the wrinkles you lose in the process are often what gave the
original work their special character.

There is no formula for this. From all accounts, Orson Welles fascist-
dress 'Julius Caesar' in the 1930s added dimensionality to Shakespeare's
play and there was more gain than loss. Tyrone Guthrie's "Troilus and
Cressida" is another instance of a contemporization which amplified
the original work. We've all seen updated Shakespeares which have
been reductive and execrable. I'm not saying it can't be done. What
I'm saying is that it requires an immense amount of taste and an understanding that it's a trade-off. You lose some things, you gain others
and in every instance, the profit and loss is going to be different.

But is there really a difference between the original meaning of

Shakespeare's plays and what actors convey to modern audiences? I know that in Elizabethan and Jacobean times, the issues were different and those audiences made topical connections that are probably beyond us, but underneath all of that there's a bedrock of emotions, relationships, pecking orders, etc that don't fundamentally change. If that is so, what's to prevent us from simply doing them according to our own lights?

You're right. Ultimately, if the plays speak to *us*, we can make them speak to modern audiences and the timelessness of the plays are reaffirmed. But how often does one see Shakespeare performed badly? How often are we shortchanged in the theatre? How many times do we leave a Shakespearean production thinking: that was only a fragment of the play compared to the fullness of the original work.

No production can deliver all the goods. Every production is always going to be partial. There's no such thing as getting a version of a classic which realizes all the multitude of possibilities that reside in a particular work. If it's a dark rendering, it won't be light. If it's public, it wont be private. If it's Expressionist, it won't be naturalistic. And that's as it should be. Every time a classic is trotted out, we should get a different beam of light shining through the kaleidoscope. And every time, the work is sound and not silly, truly innovative and not merely exploitative, we do.

That's the ideal situation. The *actual* situation is that the actor's informality, his technical deficiencies and his lack of size continually fall short of the classic's demands and so mountains are reduced to molehills just to enable actors to climb them.

But how far one can go with a classic? I agree there's got to be a certain respect for the essence of the piece, or why not do an entirely different play? But there are lots of adapters and directors who have radically transformed these plays; mixed contemporary prose with Elizabethan poetry, rearranged structure, compressed characters and forced the plays to say things that no one ever expected them to say. Are you implying all these radical restructurings are wrong?

The short answer is you can do anything you like with Shakespeare. The marble, in the hands of contemporary artists, has become clay and can be molded into whatever shape you please. But no matter how far the new adaptation departs from the original, there still has to be, as it were, radio-contact maintained with the play that bears its name. It has to cast light on something in the original work. Even if it forces us seriously to reappraise ideas originally expressed, it is still valid as a spin-off. I am much more predisposed to a free adaptation which clearly bounces off the original and never pretends to be merely an 'interpretation' of same. When Stoppard invents a "Rosencrantz and Guildenstern Are Dead" or Edward Bond writes his own treatment of 'Lear' or Brecht gives us his own version of a John Gay play or a re-structuring of "Coriolanus," we know exactly where we are. It is a no-holds'-barred deviation from the original work and we can accept it as a new work in its own right. But when adapter-directors clog the plays with alien ideas and substitute-characters to suit their 'conceptions,' we are often in neither a new place nor an old. In fact, we are in that afore-mentioned situation where Shakespeare is being exploited for the sake of someone else's agenda.

If you're going to 'take on' Shakespeare and consciously dispute his work in a work of your own, that seems to me viable and even honor-able. If you're going to change him for willful reasons and still pretend you're presenting Shakespeare, I would guess it's as dubious as trying to change the character of a boyfriend or a girlfriend or someone you marry. So: there is virtually nothing you cannot do to Shakespeare, however, your result is going to be measured by a Shakespearean yard-stick, and that's only right.

Will the American actor, do you think, ever come to terms with Shakespeare? Will he ever lose his inferiority complex in regard to those roles? Will he ever feel they belong to him as much as they do to the British actor?

Forrest did, and Junius Brutus Booth and Edwin Booth, and John Barrymore and Walter Hampden and E.H. Southern and Julia Marlowe and Richard Mansfield and Maurice Evans and Jacob Adler. People tend to forget that when the American acting tradition began in the 18th century, it began largely with Shakespeare and that Shakespeare is a very much older influence than Eugene O'Neill, the writer from whom the academicians tend to date the origins of the American theatre.

We've got Shakespeare in our bloodstream just as much as the British do and, comparatively speaking, he entered very much earlier into our national history than he did for the English. In 1752, at Williamsburgh, Virginia, the first play performed in America by a reg-ular company of actors was 'THE MERCHANT OF VENICE.' And, there's a great affinity between Shakespeare and the American charac-ter. We, like Shakespeare's characters, are athletic, passionate, impul-sive, sentimental, operating from our solar-plexus rather than our cerebrums. The patriotism in the Histories connects up with our own jingoism. We instinctively understand Othello's marital problems as we do Iago's frustration about not rising in the ranks. Our own bantering, wisecracking language corresponds to the veiled bitchiness of Beatrice and Benedict; our own ruthlessness and astrological dread is echoed in "Macbeth." The brutality of our inner-city lives overloaded as they are with tabloid horrors and acts of mayhem, mirror the brutality of a play like "Titus Andronicus." We still fall in love the way Romeo and Juliet did and nourish secret lusts as Angelo did for Isabella. In short, we understand Shakespeare in our gut.

We have the sensibility that Shakespeare needs and lack only the technique. Classical diction is a language just different enough from American speech to make us feel awkward when we adopt it, but it's a language that is not far removed from our natural speech patterns. We have to acquire formality and that sense of larger design that characterizes the best of Shakespeare's work and, most importantly, we have to learn that truthfulness and naturalism are not necessarily interchangeable; that the assumption of style is a predicate of all plays, not only classics, but that in the case of classics, it is indispensable. We have to stop taking great works of art and adapting them to our insufficiency. We have to rise to the occasion - and stop believing that in the case of classics to stoop is to conquer. It isn't; it's just to stoop.

"The Marowitz Hamlet",   Aarhus, Denmark

SHAKESPEARIAN DICTION

One of the greatest inventions of the Renaissance was the English language. Of course, there was an English language of sorts before the reign of Queen Elizabeth and the emergence of William Shakespeare, but only in the 16th century did it acquire muscularity, novelty, vigor and amplitude. The theatre, more than any other institution, popularized the new language and Shakespeare, more than any other writer (with the possible exceptions of Marlowe and Jonson) helped fashion that language into a weapon of subtlety and precision.

Plays were linguistic constructs - part of a burgeoning tradition of prosody which had begun when the dark ages were flooded by the light of the new era. The verse-forms, many of them crude and inchoate, were already in existence - awaiting the innovations of the Elizabethan authors to give them new life.

To approach Shakespeare without a knowledge of the literary conventions he utilized is to ignore a major portion of the verbal technology which he employed in writing his plays. This is not, as one might assume, merely the business of the critic or the academician. It vitally concerns the actor, for in recognizing the plays' literary characteristics, he acquires structural information which is invaluable to interpretation. The play-analyses of most actors begin and end with text and sub-text, but merely to say 'text' in regard to Shakespeare's plays without recognizing the variety of conventions available to the playwright in creating that text, is like saying that all literature, after Gutenberg, is just so much printing.

I am not referring here to the different genres such as sonnets, eclogues, epic verse, pastorals, etc. but rather to recurring patterns-of-diction which have like-characteristics and can be found throughout the canon. What follows is merely a list of some of these recurring characteristics. I am in no way attempting a scholarly exegesis on Renaissance literary forms. Several categories overlap and there may well be others which have eluded me that others will be able to identify.

PUBLIC DICTION

e.g. The Opening Court Scene and the Duel Scene in HAMLET; the opening scenes of RICHARD II and KING LEAR; The Duke's designation of Angelo as Deputy in MEASURE FOR MEASURE, The Forum Scene in JULIUS CAESAR, The Capitol scenes (II, 2) from CORIOLANUS, etc.

In all these scenes, Shakespeare adopts a tone of formality employing a heightened diction (sometimes referred to as "high" style) appropriate to ceremonial or public occasions. The scenes are often, as in "Hamlet," "Lear" and "Richard II" expository. The language is statesmanlike and somewhat exalted. It sets the scene. It involves primary characters. Often, it declares or implies a theme which is, or will become, central to the play. It eschews intimacy and seems to be directed to large assemblies - even when (as in the Court Scene in "Hamlet") individual characters are addressing one another on matters of a personal nature. There is something almost bureaucratic about the language and to do it full justice, it needs to be played in a somewhat heightened manner. Coming as it often does at the beginning of plays, it may well have been a conscious device to wrest the attention of a meandering, milling-about Elizabethan public; the verbal equivalent of a drum-roll and a flourish of trumpets.

RHETORICAL HIGHS

Lear's Storm-scene, III, 3; Othello's "Soft you; a word or two before you go...." V.2; Henry's "Once more unto the breach," III, 1: Saint Crispin's Day speech from HENRY V; Prospero's farewell to magic, "Ye elves of hills, brooks, standing lakes and groves" V, 1.

Usually the result of intensified feeling, expressed when characters are approaching an emotional climax - either lyrical or dramatic. Also moments of supreme self-awareness when the scope of what is being felt can no longer be restrained by functional blank verse and spirals upward into poetry. Rhetoric, in Shakespeare's time, had none of the pejorative sense that we associate with the word. It was neither 'hollow speech' nor 'bombastic', but intended to persuade. It travelled from public oratory to the law and eventually, to the stage. When Shakespeare employs it, it is usually charged with moral fervor, a legacy perhaps from its political and legal origins.

One has to be careful that elevated speech doesn't become inflated discourse. The actor, has to muster the feelings that justify this higher utterance, but he also has to be aware that frequently, it is the language itself which expresses them and if there is too great an intensity, the words are swallowed by the feelings.

WORD-PLAY

Capering, ostensibly improvisational dialogue characterized by puns and playful figures of speech, sometimes called 'tropes,' Often encountered in comedy-scenes especially in the mouths of clowns, but just as apparent in the exchanges of Beatrice and Benedict, Petruchio and Kate, Mercutio and Benvolio, Rosencrantz, Guildenstern and Hamlet. By-play in which characters are demonstrating their cleverness and ebullience, or acting as mouthpieces for an author who is likewise engaged.

Much of this word-play is Shakespeare showing off and it is usual for actors to use it to make their characters show off. It is hard fully to integrate these passages into the body of the work as often, they are expressly there to entertain at the expense of the play. Shakespeare often got drunk on language and when, for instance in MACBETH, II, 2, he lists seven proliferating metaphors for "sleep" ("...the innocent sleep/Sleep that knits up the ravell'd sleeve of care/The death of each day's life, sore labour's bath/Balm of hurt minds, great nature's second course/Chief nourisher in life's feast, ") apart from noting the fact that the playwright is running off at the mouth, all an actor can do, unless he introduces cuts, is to roll with the redundancies. A very special problem in Shakespeare, and one very rarely taken into account, is how to cope with his overwriting. Jonson hit the nail right on the head when he observed: "I remember the players have often mentioned it as an honour to Shakespeare that in his writing (whatsoever he penn'd) he never blotted out a line. My answer hath been would he had blotted a thousand." The practice of judiciously trimming Shakespeare seems to me to need no justification.

RUSTIC INTERLUDES & COMMONPLACES

Gardener's Scene RICHARD II, Silvius & Phoebe III,5, AS YOU LIKE IT, The Mechanicals' Scenes from MIDSUMMER NIGHT'S DREAM, Scenes with Nym, Bardolph & Pistol in HENRY V and MERRY WIVES OF WINDSOR, etc.

Scenes depicting country-types intended to be played in regional accents or city-interludes involving simple, working-class characters. Often employed by Shakespeare as part of the sub-plots running beneath the travails of his main characters or commenting thereon. They also provide 'common man' contrasts to the activities of more high-born characters. In England, it is fairly clear when a rustic scene or a city interlude appears, but in America, one is often presented with the odd spectacle of peasants or low-bred townspeople being played in plangent Shakespearean language as if they were members of the Court. By recognizing the lower social status of these characters and playing them accordingly, the diversity of Shakespeare's diction is observed and the plays achieve the intended variety.

DESCRIPTIVE SET PIECES

Cassius' description of saving Caesar's life in the Tiber; Enobarbus describing Cleopatra's voyage down the Nile; Macbeth's reflection on encountering the sleeping grooms before Duncan's murder; Gertrude's description of Ophelia's drowning; The Player King's speech about Priam and Hecuba.

Here, Shakespeare is paying homage to the earlier, highly descriptive, euphuistic style of Sir Philip Sidney, Edmund Spenser and Sir Walter Raleigh that Shakespeare grew up with and which were popular in his time. There is a feeling of ostentation about these 'set-pieces,' as if the author wanted to demonstrate a skill which he knew he possessed in spades and which he also knew would go down well with his public. Often, you see Shakespeare matching wits with his predecessors and his rivals, when, for instance in "Troilus and Cressida", he describes Helen with extended hyperbolic imagery such as: "a Grecian queen, whose youth and freshness/Wrinkles Apollo's, and makes stale the morning..../... a pearl/Whose price hath launch'd above a thousand ships/And turn'd crowned kings to merchants." We clearly hear the playwright matching his muscle with Marlowe's descriptions of Helen in "Dr. Faustus." And when in RICHARD II, he gives the King lines such as: "Was this face/Did keep ten thousand men? Was this the face/That like the sun did make beholders wink?/Was this the face that fac'd so many follies/And was at last out-fac'd by Bolingbroke?," it hard not to see Shakespeare consciously striving to out-Marlowe Marlowe with his own 'mighty lines,' I do not suggest that the actor try to play his discovery of these poetic antecedents, for clearly that would serve no dramatic purpose. But realizing that there are strains in the verse in which the playwright is conjuring up earlier poetic material, provides an historical insight which may color his interpretation.

CONCEITS

From RICHARD II, John O'Gaunt's speech "This royal throne of kings, this sceptred isle, etc" II, 1; Richard's speech, "I have been studying how I may compare/this prison where I live unto the world" 1V, 5; & Richard's "Of comfort no man speak.let us sit upon the ground/.and tell sad stories of the death of kings" III, 2; Ulysses speech about 'degree' in in I, 3 of TROILUS & CRESSIDA; Mercutio's "Queen Mab" speech from ROMEO AND JULIET; Seven Ages of man in AS YOU

LIKE IT; The Duke's meditation on death in MEASURE FOR MEASURE, "Reason thus with life; if I do lose thee, I do lose a thing/that none but fools would keep;" Polonius's advice to Laertes before his son's departure.

A compressed philosophical idea often illustrating a truism, but so eloquently put that the language alone is its reason-for-being. Or a sustained flight of fancy which constitutes a theme-and-variations around a central motif. Often in the body of soliloquies, they are also to be found within scenes when characters, deeply stirred, strain for either a paradigm or a metaphor in which to crystallize their thoughts. Occasionally, it takes the form of a kind of moralizing laundry-list as it does with Polonius talking to Laertes before his departure to France, or a chronological inventory, as in the Seven Ages of Man speech. Sometimes it is an elaborate metaphor about Country, as it is in John O'Gaunt's "other Eden" speech in RICHARD II or a peroration on Death as it is in MEASURE FOR MEASURE when the disguised Duke tries to reconcile Claudio to his fate. But in most of these instances, it is Shakespeare off on a riff, consciously using language to poetically extend an idea which has caught his fancy.

LYRICAL EXCHANGES

The expression of intensely felt personal emotion usually of a tender or amorous nature and, in Shakespeare, often embellished with antique allusions. The exchanges between Romeo and Juliet are probably the most representative examples but the beginning of V,1 in THE MERCHANT OF VENICE ("The moon shines bright; in such a night as this...etc") is another prime example as is Troilus and Cressida's first meeting (III,2). Lyricism, in Shakespeare, is often a reversion to

Elizabethan romanticism; a conjuration of the spirit (and often the letter) of poets such as Sir Thomas Wyatt, George Gascoigne and Thomas Campion. To appreciate the flavor of that lyricism, it helps to relate those scenes to the poetry that influenced them.

TWISTS OF IRONY

Shakespeare often uses irony en passant, but occasionally, he entirely saturates a speech with it and then it is like a strong, primary color which, though diffused with other colors, conspicuously shines through. Shylock's reply to Antonio's request for the loan is a clear example of this quality ("Signor Antonio, many a time and oft in the Rialto..."). As is Richard II's response to Bolingbroke in III, 3 "We are amaz'd; and thus long have we stood/To watch the fearful bending of thy knee...etc." RICHARD III is littered with such twists - witness Richard's speech I,3 which begins: "Was ever woman in this humour woo'd?/Was ever woman in the humour won?" Such ironies are often shared with the audience as a dimension of the character's nature which is usually concealed from others. Think of the barbed irony in Iago's soliloquies to the audience about the progress of his plot against Othello or Petruchio's confidences to the audience about his strategies in taming Kate.

APOSTROPHE

Marc Anthony's "Oh judgment, thou art fled to brutish beasts" and the speech that begins: "Oh pardon me, thou bleeding piece of earth." Queen Margaret's curse against Gloucester in I, 3 of RICHARD III: "If heaven any grievous plague in store/Exceeding those that I can wish upon thee", Lear in I, 4, bringing his curse down upon Goneril's head: "Hear, Nature., hear! dear goddess hear!/Suspend thy purpose, if thou didst intend/To make this creature fruitful! Into her womb convey steril-ity!", Edmund's soliloquy: "Thou Fortune, art my goddess; Constance in III, 4: "Death of death; O, amiable lovely death!/Thou odoriferous stench! sound rotten-ness!" etc.

Often in Shakespeare, characters invoke the gods, address absent persons or call upon some generalized abstract power. In such mo-ments, the focus shifts away from the immediate and towards some more metaphysical sphere. In Shakespeare's time, direct access to such supernatural powers was believed to be possible, and characters often addressed them. Invariably, the language of such exhortations is more charged and potent than the social diction from which they spring. In Lear, for instance, when the King visits Goneril, the scene begins with a small, familial altercation, but Lear is soon blazing with divine fire. When the apostrophe occurs, Lear shifts his focus from Albany to ex-hort the heavens to make Goneril barren and, as the pressure increases on the old man, the language increases in intensity. At the height of it, Lear is discoursing with those very elements which will shortly blow him every-which-way in the Heath Scene and sunder his majesty once and for all. Yes, it is a kind of dramatic climax, but its form is apostro-phe and the actor knowing that, has a literary signpost to direct him to a theatrical effect.

PARODY

.Players Scene HAMLET, III, 2; Pyramus & Thisbe V, 1, MIDSUMMER NIGHT'S DREAM; "The rugged Pyrrhus, he whose sable arm," HAMLET II, 2 etc.

Occasionally Shakespeare makes a direct allusion to an earlier theatrical convention which would have been immediately recognizable to his own audience. The stilted verse of the Play Scene in HAMLET, apart from its use as a dramatic device in the Prince's conspiracy against Claudius, is clearly a throwback to an earlier form of doggerel drama suggesting the Miracle and Mystery Plays of the 14th and 15th centuries. The Player King's speech about Pyrrhus and Hecuba conjures up the kind of heroic drama that Elizabethan audiences were still lapping up in Shakespeare's time. Often, to concretize points which have previously been made in blank verse, he will resort to rhyme as in RICHARD II, (V, 3) where the Duchess of York pleads to Bolingbroke to pardon her son. ("Forever will I walk upon my knees/And never see day that the happy sees/Till thou give joy; until thou bid me joy/By pardoning Rutland, my transgressing boy.") At such moments, when rhyme encapsulates a character's emotional state, it is as if some vestigial memory in Shakespeare recalls the rhyming patterns of the old Mystery plays and the playwright involuntarily slips into the earlier convention. This is a very different motivation from the scenes between Lysander, Helen, Demetrius and Hermia in MIDSUMMMER NIGHT'S DREAM where rhyme is a conscious factor in conveying the comedy imbroglios. The contemporary custom is always to side-step the rhyming-pattern and avoid the end-stopped lines, but there are occasions, as in Richard Wilbur's translations of Moliere, where a head-on assault on the rhyme can be equally as effective.

SOLILOQUY

Sometimes direct addresses to the audience (as in the Chorus of HENRY V, RICHARD III's opening speech in the eponymous play) but more often, private streams of consciousness whose focus is inward. The richness and variety of Shakespearean soliloquies do not lend themselves to generalization. The crucial thing is to find where the focus of the speech is: the audience, the heavens, the nether world, or internally - to a past event, a prospect in the future, or a shuttling between two points (as it is for Claudius in The Prayer Scene ("O, my offence is rank") or Hamlet in the speech that follows ("Now might I do it pat"). In both those speeches, there is a shuttling between apostrophe and meditation. The overriding problem is how to integrate familiar soliloquies into the actions which either precede or follow them, so they do not feel like disconnected audition-pieces or set arias.

Knowing that Shakespeare has composed a set-piece, a run of descriptive verse, an allegory or an intellectual conceit doesn't take the actor off the hook as far as motivation and sub-text are concerned. He still has to find ways to connect the literary convention with the weave of his character and the needs of the scene, but knowing that part of the author's intention is contained in a conscious literary form is an additional piece of information that may influence how he deals with that particular section of text. If, for instance, the actress playing Gertrude is unaware that her description of Ophelia's drowning is as much a poem about the young girl's death as it is an emotional conjuration of the event, she may simply saturate the verse in shock and horror, delivering the sort of breathless report that you or I might give of a fatal traffic-accident we have just witnessed. But once the literary motivation of the speech is comprehended (along with its dramatic function), she may decide to objectify the words in a way she would not have done otherwise.

Of course any one can play any thing any way they like, if they can make it work, but in probing the text and looking for clues to interpretation, it seems foolhardy to ignore clear-cut indications that, at such-and-such a point, the author was indulging in a conscious piece of literary construction. Sometimes the author's motivation has to take primacy over the character's because sometimes Shakespeare is using his creations simply as a mouthpiece for his own authorial devices. The actor may decide to ignore these signposts, to integrate everything into his character's mix and the thrust of the dramatic situation. That is a perfectly legitimate decision. It only becomes questionable if the actor doesn't *realize* the author's extra-theatrical intentions; if he tramples set-pieces and conceits, parodies and descriptive verse because he is unaware of their literary constituents.

To draw attention to these conscious literary constructions, it is sometimes useful to excerpt the excerptable sections of a play; that is, to find self-contained units of descriptive verse, set-pieces or rhetorical highs and extract them from the body of the work and, during rehearsals, perform them in isolation. Once the structure of these 'parts' are fully understood, and why they have been placed there, they must be seamlessly integrated into the whole. Having been consciously extracted and alienated from their context, the actor's challenge becomes: how do I restore them to their proper place and create the flow which renders them organic? This is particularly delicate in the case of highly familiar speeches and soliloquies which already obtrude from their context and draw attention to themselves. The removal of these 'parts' from the 'whole' often provides technical insights into prosody, scansion and style which generalized rehearsal neglects. By becoming aware of 'literary pattern' in one place, the actor sometimes finds similar patterns recurring elsewhere - for Shakespeare was nothing if not a pattern-maker. But one must reiterate: the point of particularizing the verse in this way is to master its structure and then reintegrate the pieces into the whole. A situation not unlike a violinist repeatedly practicing a difficult cadenza in a concerto before being able to play it smoothly and effortlessly within its original score.

Those that contend that the canon is essentially language and the way to convey it is simply to master the language, tend to be blind to the richness of the plays' intrinsic imagery and mythology. Those that belittle the demands of the language or believe they can go directly to the play's dramatic essence without assimilating their literary structure are like people who are constantly felled by obstacles because they never recognize they are there. It is the language which evokes the imagery and stirs the mythology, and the paradox is that it's only by coming to terms with the nuts and bolts of Shakespeare's words that the larger, magnificent machine can be activated.

Of all the Elizabethan writers, Shakespeare was the most avant-garde. He consciously toyed with conventions which many of his contemporaries treated with stiff-necked respect. Like any good avant-gardist, he employed parody and satire and cocked his snook at established practices. When Polonius begins to explain to Claudius his theory of Hamlet's madness: "My liege, and madam, to expostulate/

What majesty should be, what duty is/ Why day is day, night night, and time is time/ Were nothing but to waste night, day and time./ Therefore since brevity is the soul of wit/And tediousness the limbs and outward flourishes,/ I will be brief. - Your noble son is mad." - Polonius is taking the piss out of a whole set of stuffy grammarians and writers such as John Marston who epitomized the musclebound, didactic style that Shakespeare cooly dismantled. One can appreciate Polonius' euphuistic diction without knowing anything about its actual target, but realizing the parodic subtext unquestionably confers an added dimension.

It is one of the theatre's great ironies that one of the freest and most innovative authors of the 17th century is so often pedanticized by people who never recognize him for the libertine he actually was.

*   *   *   *   *

LUNATIC, LOVER, AND POET

"The lunatic, the lover, and the poet,
Are of imagination all compact."
'Midsummer Night's Dream'

The actor's most essential task is the construction of his character's state of mind. It is the latitude and longitude of that state-of-mind which ultimately determines the scope, style, bearing and depth of his portrayal. Having conceived it and then cobbled it together through trial and error, his next essential task is to take up residence there.

The psychotic is also in a 'state of mind' - usually not one of his own making, but imposed upon him by unfortunate psychic circumstances. The actor and the psychotic are alike in one special regard: they both play out the images and actions of the mental worlds they inhabit; both, social extensions of body-regulating mental conditions .

The actor, like the psychotic, is subject to a delusion about his character and his world. In the psychotic, the unconscious has taken the upper hand and organized everything around a false reality. The actor, on the other hand, consciously manipulates consciousness in order to engender psychosis, goading his unconscious into directions alien to his true nature. The psychotic beds down and rises up with delirium. The actor, uses his powers of concentration and imagination in order to conjure it up consciously. The actor's hold on character is fragile, transient, constantly trying to achieve consistency within a set of changing psychological circumstances. The psychotic who believes he is Napoleon or Lincoln or Jesus Christ is 'in character' in a way that the actor can never be; although the actor is striving for exactly that state of total identification.

The psychotic, like the actor, employs a double consciousness. He is unwaveringly certain in his deluded state and has only a dim awareness of the reality which has abandoned him. He straddles between the real and the imaginary, the latter constantly transforming the former. The psychotic is the victim of his double consciousness but the actor is the master of his. He is like a man on a tightrope inhabiting one stratosphere but constantly viewing another below it. Maintaining balance consists of mastering the space between his loft above and the ground below - functioning in one while maintaining a dim but necessary awareness of the other. The psychotic is, in a sense, the perfect tightrope-walker - except that he can never come down to *terra firma*. The actor wavers and oscillates, agonizes every precarious next step, worrying whether his right foot is sufficiently rooted to allow his left foot to carry him one step further. Double consciousness is the knack which sustains his art, the contradiction that maintains his equilibrium.

The psychotic's belief in illusion is total. It does not permit of any doubt. The actor's contrived illusion is constantly being questioned, subverted, dissected, striving to be more plausible, more efficacious. The conscious mind is constantly weighing his illusion in order to make it more cohesive, more fool-proof. Think of the actor who has almost but not quite learned his lines, shuttling between continuity and forgetfulness, lapsing out of character just long enough to ask for his cue or confirm a piece of blocking, nakedly revealing the mechanisms by which his character is being methodically assembled. *There* is the perfect example of the schizoid personality - someone who is simultaneously Self and Other; one personality constantly segueing into another. The psychotic however, suffers no such schism; the immersion in his imaginary circumstances is total. His belief-system is never threatened by doubts or reappraisal. He is always 'in character.'

What am I saying? That madmen make the best actors? No, almost the opposite - that the actor, by means of a heightened act of sanity, must balance consciousness and imagination in order to delude himself, and others, into the reality he is trying to simulate. However, without the psychotic's belief in the unreal, the wholesale acceptance of illusions which lead to *his* being deluded, the actor will always be throwing logs on a fire that never ignites. A kind of temporary insanity, if you like, is the flame which ultimately enkindles that wood and makes the fire roar, and every good actor enters into a state of mania when he succeeds in convincing us, and himself, of his imaginary circumstances. It is the 'normal' actor whose every step is calculated, as obvious to him as it is to us, that gives the worst performances. His sanity is never in question and, because his disbelief, unlike the psychotic's, is never truly suspended, neither is ours.

The psychotic, like the actor, forces us to adjust to his peculiar brand of mania. When dealing with a madman, our sanity is useless. We must retire it and adopt a demeanor and manner of speech which accommodates the patient; the same applies when we are speaking to a child. Our cynicism, our irony, our subtlety is of no avail when the person with whom we are communicating is denied that frame-of-reference which enables cynicism, irony and subtlety to register. We 'adjust' to psychotics - just as the actor adjusts to his playing-partner.

Indeed, adjustment is the golden mien by which acting takes place. An actor who does not adjust to his changing situation and the characters he encounters cannot be said to be acting; or at least, not very well, since, being out of touch, he neglects those minute connections between himself and others that creates the contact (the magic circle) which draws the spectators into the fictional circumstances. By *adjusting* to the actor's temporary madness, his fellow-actors assimilate his 'mania' just as normal people create a modus operandi with the insane. When doing so, we subscribe to a world-view which is not ours but which we must adopt if we are to be in communication at all.

The other relevant parallel here is danger. Psychotics because they are in a realm of their own and not subject to the objective criteria which guide the conduct of 'normal people,' are potentially dangerous. We do not know what they will do next. We have no basis for predicting the logical behavior of a character who, unlike ourselves, subscribes to no shared idea of logic. So even as we are drawn into the psychotic's orbit in order to relate to him or her, it is with the utmost apprehension.

In acting, we are continually talking about taking risks' about 'dangerous performers' - and always commendably. The risk-taking actor who is 'dangerous' appeals to us much more than the staid actor who simply 'goes through the motions' and is consequently, 'predictable.' It is *un*predictability, and *dangerous unpredictability* at that, which essentially captures our imagination in the theatre - and again, it is a quality peculiar to the psychotic state.

There is a long-standing connection between 'inspiration' and 'madness' and history is littered with allusions to 'inspired madmen' -

just as the history of theatre is filled with examples of actors who, in an excess of inspiration, severed the bonds that usually attach them to reason. Acting encourages both inspiration and madness because it is constantly prodding the actor out of his settled norm and into regions far removed from those common to his actor's psyche. An extreme version of this is the actor who, having played Othello a thousand times, identifies so strongly with the role that he is capable of strangling his wife in a fit of jealousy, or an actor so enveloped by the character of Lear that he allows the pressures that beset the old man to dismantle his own reason.

By 'acting-out' his profoundest anti-social impulses over and over again, the actor releases something in his own psyche which, normally suppressed, assumes an outward shape in his personal life. His 'mania' if you like, becomes practiced and biologically embedded. Ordinarily, a fictitious characterization doesn't transform the actor who adopts it, but life is always imitating art, and there are innumerable instances of actors whose 'personalities' were conditioned by the roles they played; who, in a sense, became social extensions of their dramatic personae. And not only in extreme cases. Think of bland, blasé, upper middle-class Englishmen who carried the practiced gentility found in Noel Coward's plays into their own lives or aggressive young actors whose social-selves tended to reflect the sour, irascible, malcontents they portrayed in the era of the 'angry young man.' In the first category, there is a whole stratum of people who can be said to have emulated and then simulated the social demeanor and mind-sets of characters in Coward's drawing-room comedies; suave, dry, emotionally-brittle types untouched by the vulgarity of passions or the embarrassment of outburst; in the second, actors such as Kenneth Haigh, Albert Finney, Tom Bell and Nicol Willamson whose personal lives were mingled with strands from the plays they performed. Perhaps the most conspicuous examples are to be drawn from films of the 50s. How many young men of the period owed the stamp of their social personalities to the Marlon Brandos and Jimmy Deans upon whom they consciously or unconsciously modeled their inner selves? How many strong, silent, he-man types today secretly pattern themselves on Clint Eastwood?

Actors cast spells. Acting is magic. Not only does it use greasepaint, lighting and costume to create plausible illusions, it also releases a certain demoniac energy into the auditorium which infects the minds and imaginations of those exposed to it. The ancients believed implicitly in the power of acting to transform others. "The Muse first of all inspires men herself," wrote Plato in the Ion "and from these inspired persons a chain of other persons is suspended who take the inspiration." In Joseph Roach's book *The Player's Passion*, he cites a 19th century authority who wrote "that fictitious sufferings sometimes lead to real infirmities, and sometimes death. Pliny recorded that an actor once imitated the symptoms of gout with such verisimilitude that he thereby contracted the disease. Seneca related the frightening case of Gallus Vibius, who went mad while rehearsing the part of a madman."

The energy generated by the actor and transmitted to the audience is identical to that evoked by shamans, witch-doctors and spiritualists. It is not make-believe energy or simulated energy; it has the same psychic constituents that are to be found in madmen, persons of heightened sensitivity or people in the throes of powerful emotion. What is being stirred in all these cases is blood, not stage-blood, and so when we look for instruction as to how to create these states in ourselves, it behooves us to examine those persons in whom the blood roars the loudest and the transformation of Self is the most total.

Transcendence of self is a necessary condition of characterization;

even in those cases where, as the Stanislavskyites argue, a close parallel exists between the actor's personality and that of the character. You may pattern your performance of Hamlet on your own personal melancholia and vacillation, but you still have to plant yourself in Shakespearean terrain, period considerations and an imaginative 'otherness' in order to play the role. The actor who does not escalate from his mundane, 20th century modernity into the poetic world visualized by the dramatist never makes that necessary ascent from actor to character. The more demanding the play, the further the distance the actor has to travel out of himself towards his appointed, artistic destination. But even when perfectly cast in a character whose characteristics mirror one's own, the art of acting demands a geographical excursion from the actor's world to the playwright's, a shift from Real Time to Stage Time. Since getting out of one's self and into another Self is the inescapable imperative of acting and since it is essentially a transformation of psychologies which is involved, the true actor is one who is able to put his head into another place; who can so manipulate his personal sanity that it transfuses itself into another's. Acting, when it succeeds, is an out-of-mind and out-of-body experience and there is no contradiction in the fact that while it is happening, the audience is watching the mind-and-body of the actor who has translated himself elsewhere. The theatre is the Here-and-Now at the service of the Then-and-There and it is the simultaneity of those opposites that makes it magical.

We encounter this mania in familiar social situations. We all know people who suffer from delusions of grandeur, who are figments of their own imagination, who maintain a mythical notion of themselves which does not correspond to objective criteria and consequently, appear obnoxious or pathetic in the eyes of others. What are such people doing but 'acting out' images of themselves based on imaginary or inflated conceptions, and what is it the actor does who must essay Caesar or Shylock or Timon? He must project a dimensionality of character - either grand or craven or misanthropic - far removed from the mundane molecules of his own personality. We do not say of actors portraying great kings or tyrants that they are suffering from 'delusions of grandeur;' rather, we assess the lineaments of their delusion to see if they are consistent, compelling and effective. But the mechanism by which the actor becomes grandiose is precisely the same as that which inflates ordinary people who entertain extraordinary notions of themselves. It is a departure from the norm; a deviation into abnormal behavior - which is precisely what acting is - for even the basic assumption that one is pretending to be someone else is a deviation from the norm and involves the adoption of anti-social behavior. It is only the convention of the playhouse and the suspended disbelief of the audience that renders this deviation permissible. Outside the playhouse, in a restaurant or a church, we would find such behavior intolerable. We would say of such people that they are 'mad' and 'ought to have their head examined.' Psychotics should *indeed* have their head examined - but once examined, one would find the same allegiance to privately-constructed belief-systems that characterize actors simulating people they are *not*, in circumstances far removed from those which constitute their norm. The madman is the existential actor. The man who turns all society into an audience for himself and who persists in his lunatic integrity no matter what objections are thrown up to contradict him. Is the actor who insists for the length of an evening's performance that he is a scheming villain, a murderous tyrant or a besotted lover so very different?

Psychiatrists tell us that schizophrenics abound with energy and insights. From the labyrinth of their specialized perceptions, they often

see things not granted to normal people. The palettes of their imagination are so suffused with colors that, in contrast, those who minister
to them appear to inhabit a drab, monochromatic world. Yet when we
act, it is precisely for that galaxy of colored effects that we strive; those
unexpected juxtapositions of emotion; those fluctuating highs and lows
of elation and despair which, outside the theatre we label manic-de-
pression. Hamlet, having seen his father's ghost, shuttles between ex-
ultation and paranoia, resolve and dread, fortitude and fancy. "These
are but wild and whirling words, my Lord," says Horatio. The madness
of Hamlet is like the temporary madness of the sane actor. He too, in
deciding to feign madness, has to try to toe the line between two mental states; he too, sometimes lapses from one into the other. 'Is Hamlet
mad or sane' is not the question that we should be asking; rather, what
are the parameters of Hamlet's sanity which induce him occasionally to
step beyond them, and are those moments of 'insanity' any different
from the mania all actors (i.e. people feigning people they are not) experience when their desires carry them to emotional extremes?

If by madness we mean the suspension of our own sensibilities and
the colonization of ourselves by foreign or alien beings, then the actor
must, to some extent or other, become a madman. The fact that this
madness is achieved through a highly sophisticated intellectual process,
doesn't alter the fact that its goal is a transformation of personal identity. Medical scientists have been known to inject toxins into their system in order to unravel the mysteries of diseases for which they were
seeking a cure. The actor, like the risk-taking scientist, does the same
thing when he turns himself into an organism invaded by a foreign
body. Just as the scientist takes precautions against total infection, so
does the actor guard against permanent transformation - but the scientist who declines such risks, like the actor who refuses to stretch his sen-

sibility to the utmost, cannot help but circulate endlessly on beaten paths and become staled by custom.

*   *   *   *   *

OTHERNESS

When I started in the theatre, I believed a director was the chess-master, the stage the board and the actors, the chess-pieces. In my mind, the actors' prime function was to delineate a preconceived pattern of the director's making. The hardest thing, I found as a director, was getting actors to move about the board - for I realized that every cross, every sit and every rise was an expression of some intricate inner necessity which either told the story or obfuscated it. I spent a lot of time doodling diagrams on the margins of scripts to insure that people would execute my choreography.

Most of these preparations were in vain. Invariably my actors' instincts sent them in different directions and inevitably, my master-plan would be upset by their maddening unpredictability. Gradually, I abandoned the whole notion of a master - plan and came to rehearsals with no prescribed moves at all, armed only with a grasp of what I thought the scene was about. As we worked, I allowed myself to be guided by impulses received during rehearsals - a cross here, a turn there - allowing things spontaneously to combust. I took this to be a great step forward because I had stopped directing *myself* and began instead to find the 'directions' indicated by the actors in the give-and-take of rehearsals.

It is generally agreed that the pattern-of-movement in a play is the externalization of the way a director visualizes it and, by and large, actors tend to accept the spatial relationships imposed by the director. But after I had relinquished my prerogative to work from a blueprint, I was taking my cue, not from my own preconceptions, but from what I took to be the spontaneous impulses of my actors. I was still 'directing' in that I accepted certain moves and modified others, but in a very crucial sense, the fulcrum had shifted.

As time went on, I came to realize that the natural impulse of most actors was towards what one might call conditioned social reflexes; rising to greet someone who had come into the room; pacing about to convey anxiety or confusion; slumping into a chair to express contemplation of fatigue. It was not so much that these movements were false but that they signaled emotional responses which had as much to do with ingrained stage-custom as they did the patterns of human behavior. It soon occurred to me that contrary motion or contradictory movement could be just as effective since people often moved in order to compensate for what they were feeling, and what they were feeling was usually very different from what they were saying.

Later I came to understand that behind the realm of psychology there lurked a deeper motivation, one which characters themselves were often unaware. If you dug deeply enough, you could uproot a physical pattern which stood in the same relation to social behavior as the latent content of dreams did to their manifest content. I came to see that physical movement, by and large, was a language, like verbal language, which had as many layers as the individual had secrets to hide or emotions to suppress. Behavior, far from being motion reflected in a looking-glass, was more like light refracted through a prism.

I started to reverse all of my earlier findings. Rather than accept the signal impulses which 'came naturally' to actors and actresses, I delved into what was deeper than their apparent 'natures,' seeking that which their 'natures' were avoiding or denying. As I could not accept my own first instincts in regard to the geography of the scene, so I could not accept those of the actors either. We both had to go further than our first instincts - into areas which were as clouded for them as they were for myself.

But a director, not being an actor, has not conditioned his body to ferret out and then express what is most deeply embedded in his psyche. He may divine it or probe it intellectually, but only the actor can find it kinetically; can bring it to the surface. The director's job was to provide the logistical support needed by the actor to make those self-discoveries and to reject the practiced impulses that frequently blocked the way towards unearthing what lay deeper.

It appeared that inside of every actor there was a hidden actor. Although he could occasionally be glimpsed behind language or characterization, he never wholly surfaced. He often had 'moments' or 'flashes' where certain remarkable things were glimpsed. Through exercises that transcended his normal social functioning, the hidden actor could occasionally be revealed. His uniqueness stood in striking contrast to the more conventional personage that normally negotiated on his behalf. He was much freer and uninhibited than his surface-self and in much closer contact with his deeper instincts. More essence than matter, he could nevertheless shape matter so that it became essential. Although intrinsically abstract, he was constantly looking for ways to make his abstractness concrete. When given free reign, he could transform his characters, investing them with the uniqueness of his own being. The shell of studied characteristics would split apart to reveal a fascinating human being unlike anyone else. When that hidden nature coalesced with inspiration, it brought inert material to life and the hidden actor, now revealed, astonished everyone with whom he came into contact.

How to reach that hidden actor and marshal his resources became the object of intensive labor; a task made more strenuous by the fact that no formula existed by which he could be routed out. It was as hit and miss as everything else that took place in the rehearsal-situation. But in this case, one knew what one was searching for could never be found in the superficies of rehearsal; everything in the production-procedure militated against its discovery. It was in the resourcefulness and inventiveness of the hidden actor that the surface-actor could break through and install the best part of himself on stage. But ironically, it was the timidities and anxieties of the surface-actor that created the barrier which obstructed his emergence. The prime object of rehearsals then, was to create the conditions by which the surface-actor could be usurped and the hidden actor installed. The way to bring this about depended on a delicate conjunction between director and performer. The certainty that this 'other actor' was there justified all the anguish and frustration involved in working with his superficial counterpart.

Insights about acting-chemistry threw the written word into a different perspective. Text yes, and behind that, sub-text, but what was behind that? Character yes, but from what stage in a person's life? Their adolescence, their childhood, their infancy? If the child lives on in the adult, what portion of the adult is made up of the child? What cloaking modifications have been made by the adult? At what point in the civilizing process does the savage get entirely eliminated leaving only the socially-adjusted individual? If a successful and effective black General, fiendishly manipulated into vengeance and jealousy, can turn into something primitive and murderous, does that mean that the upright General was merely a facade? Would the facade had remained in tact if the psychological pressures had never been applied? What would Hamlet have become if never prodded by the visitation of his ghostly father? Would he simply have adjusted to the new dispensation, married Ophelia, suppressed his regal ambitions, made up with his mother and settled for a cabinet post, perhaps Minister of Education, in the new regime?

All of these questions are prompted by the underlying question: what does the inner-structure of a character consist of, and to what extent should these non-manifest possibilities be taken into account in his social persona, given the fact that, under extraordinary circumstances, any one of them can rise to the surface.

If each character's personal motivation was unique unto himself, was it not false and arbitrary to try to unify them according to one man's (the director's) vision? But then, if every character was given free reign, what did that portend for the unity of the whole? Was a disparate and unvariegated result justifiable on the grounds that it more faithfully reflected the way people actually behaved? But then art, I reminded myself, was not primarily concerned with verisimilitude. The artists - playwright, director and acting-company - made their own unity in the work of art which paralleled or augmented the reality on which it was ostensibly based.

The business of rehearsals was finding things which were not immediately apparent, but if one fell into a formulaic search, it became something of a child's treasure hunt - unearthing only what had already been planted in order to be found. But what was one looking for and where in the actor's psyche and the playwright's material, did one conduct these searches? And with what tools does one carry out these investigations?

Intellectual analysis was a given - no sooner did one read a play or examine one's role than the mind began to suggest a number of interpretative possibilities. The actor could 'experience' information through improvisation and exercise which might cast light on hidden areas of the work. Then there were the leads provided by fellow-actors who, in trying to solve their own problems, threw up provocative challenges to others. One had to make sure there was an open line of communication to fellow-actors which meant reaching out to them without impeding one's own inventions. But in gainfully employing all these tools, there was an initial obstruction which had first to be removed and that was the most formidable obstacle of all.

Just as the actor had his baggage of tricks, mannerisms, short-cuts and inculcated clichés, so the director was burdened with prior assumptions, coagulated beliefs, old admirations unconsciously yearning to be duplicated - not to mention a whole storehouse of received wisdom which, once acquired tended to go unchallenged. The commencement of rehearsals was like the meeting of two magicians each balancing his own bag of tricks on his back and each assuming his was the largest and most valuable. Before one ever got to the issues of the play, one had to negotiate the smoldering but tacit demands of each participant. This involved wheedling, deviousness and dollops of child-psychology on the part of the director; treachery, elusiveness and duplicity on the part of the actor. Meanwhile the author stood by watching his work unravel and wondering if, when it was all put together again, it would ever resemble his original creation. Illusions of grandeur and premonitions of disaster hung heavy in the air. To make matters worse, the tyrannical clock forbade experiment or time spent investigating tantalizing side-turnings which, if explored, might have yielded marvels.

The attitude behind the work became defensive - to ward off those conditioned reflexes which like diseased cells prevented healthy ones from forming. A new strategy was required to avoid the old pitfalls. The notion of ur-text was considered valuable, if only because it held out the promise of life beyond sub-text. Taking an oblique path to the material via improvisation and root-exercises was also beneficial in that it widened the parameters of a written work and allowed ideas to enter its air-space from every point on the compass. As soon as one saw a play as part of a greater entity, it gave actors an opportunity to discover more ramifications than could be found in the closed-circuit work-of-art. It also reminded artists that a slice-of-life, no matter what its dimensions, had to be sliced from something greater than itself and, by identifying that larger mass, it widened the actors' scope and encouraged them to look beyond the parameters set by the playwright. The actor was raised to the level of both the playwright and the director, releasing him from his traditional subjugation to text and mise-en-scene. He was offered a major role in collaboration rather than the self-effacing role of dutiful interpreter. It also, I must admit, opened certain floodgates which encouraged egotism and idiosyncrasy to run riot — but there never is a genuine breakthrough either in art or science that doesn't carry with it the danger of abuse.

The secret at the heart of theatre — if not all art — is complexity.

By fastening onto one reductive system which seemed to explain and codify it, we were evading much larger issues. Experience was not there to be compressed into a formula but translated into as many theorems as seemed to pertain to its endless variety. The quest was not for a system or a method, but a state of mind which succeeded in capturing the theatre's ever-changing multiplicity. Systematization and methodology fostered the delusion of having cracked the nut but no one system or methodology could crack every nut. There were more nuts than there were systems to contain them.

In order to achieve the most definitive theatrical result, a technique was needed which was at least as complex as the problem. One that didn't complacently accept the notion that acting was merely projected personality and theatre, the automatic assembly of the playwright's words. It was precisely this kind of niggling dissatisfaction with prevailing standards which had inspired earlier artists to probe more deeply, to reject the familiar and the customary, the manufactured replicas and the reasonable facsimiles. Just as Stanislavsky, Brecht and Artaud had rejected the reactionary practices of their predecessors, so it was beholden upon us to challenge the implicit social and behavioral customs which ran beneath what we, parceling them off from larger indivisible things, called acting-technique. To be an actor then, meant being a critic of both art and life and, to be an effective actor, that criticism had to be converted into practical maneuvers which combated the banalities of art in order to avoid reproducing the clichés of life.

Ploddingly, through a series of stumbles and detours, collisions with stone-walls and wanderings up blind-alleys, I came to realize that the actor doesn't so much 'build a character' as step into a magnetic field where he is affected by emanations from the ideas, impulses and environment dictated by the production. He doesn't so much 'become a character' or 'live a role' as absorb actions, feelings and experiences relative to his character and, in so doing, triggers like-actions, like-feelings and like-experiences in his own being; that the actor is a conductor-of-energies *already mobilized* and ready to leap into parallel situations; that he doesn't 'perform' so much as allow the psychic functioning of his character to release universal information already bred in his bone and etched in his memory; that phylogeny precedes psychology and that the physical is only the most conspicuous aspect of the metaphysical. The whole notion of constructing a performance - brick by brick, beat by beat, choice by choice - is a bogus linear illusion fostered by over a hundred years of outworn acting theory and inculcated by a mechanistic philosophy which modern science has effectively refuted, although its residue remains lodged in the actors' mind and locked in his musculature.

The actor is not the walking duality described by thinkers as diverse as Gordon Craig, Constantin Stanislavsky, Antonin Artaud and Bertolt Brecht but a force-field where memories and habits originated in prehistory and the primordial slime, dynamically interact, and that every evolutionary development which has refined the human organism over the millenia plays *some* part and exerts *some* influence in the living present. Being an actor is not so much a question of 'training' and 'development' but of awakening susceptibilities to the play's situations, stated and implied; the playwright's intentions, latent and overt; the director's interpretation, articulated and inchoate.

What needed to be abandoned was the idea that an actor was an accretion of conscious maneuvers such as memorization, blocking and psychological intent instead of a catalytic agent which synthesized all of these things, filtering them through an acting-metabolism which enabled him to recreate past experience rooted in conscious and pre-conscious memory and which, under favorable conditions, could manifest itself. Acting was not something you 'do' but something done *to you* if you were free enough to discard clogging formulae and reductive egotism and open yourself up to a kind of eternal consciousness of which personal psychology was only the tiniest fraction.

If one recoiled from abstractions such as these and took refuge in nuts-and-bolts, in 'units and objectives,' in provable premises and common practices, one was cozying oneself into an hermetically-sealed capsule which, though it looked like the macrocosm, was actually a microcosm.

*   *   *   *

The theatre is a serial art; actors and directors go from play to play often working in very different circumstances and on highly contrasted material. Unless blessed with the continuity of a permanent ensemble working in the same venue, each production represents a new start. The insights and refinements created with a previous group of actors do not automatically transfer to a new company. One has to begin all over again and the tendency to do so tends to mechanize a process which should be ongoing and regenerative. Many of the problems thrown up by work in the theatre would either be solved or considerably reduced if the same director worked with the same actors for an extended period of time. After a while, a group intelligence is engendered which becomes greater than the director's and the actors' intelligence combined. But so long as the theatre remains an ad hoc art form, it will be necessary to formulate a modus operandi to enable it start afresh each time.

The key is to maintain a kind of flexible skepticism - a deep-seated reluctance to accept what comes too easily (often automatically) and then construe it as being 'natural.' What comes most 'naturally' to both actors and directors is the tendency to repeat themselves; to print out yet again what has been pre-programmed.

Whenever a company of actors assemble, the onus is always the same: they must for the sake of the work before them, form an ensemble, provide a gloss peculiar to themselves and their work-situation, realize a joint conception of the work in conjunction with the other members of the artistic team and resolve not to repeat what has been done before or promote novelty for its own sake. Because the theatre has to a large extent become routine, play-production has become standardized. No sooner do rehearsals begin than artists feel the pressure to deliver results. Because the text is the most tangible element in the process, it is clung to for dear life. Language is memorized, organized, physically circumscribed and, before the most elementary secrets of the play are explored or discovered, coagulated. During the process, there are gestures to characterization, allusions to sub-text and lip-service to thematic ideas, but the object of the journey is to arrive at one's destination as promptly as possible. The landscape is never glimpsed and, like suburbanites having dutifully caught the 7:04, the commuters conceal themselves behind newspapers so as to have only the most minimal contact with their fellow-passengers. When the train finally pulls in to the station, everyone goes their own way.

But the actor's journey must be the antithesis of the commuter's. There should be dialogue, discussion and the vigorous interchange of ideas all along the way. Every bit of landscape needs to be assimilated; every passing observation analyzed and disputed. On arrival, everyone should jam into the same taxi and be driven to the same address. The arrival should be thought of as the springboard for a new departure; the performance, not the pay-off of rehearsals but, the first phase of the grander journey which is the run-of-the-play.

What hampers us are age-old obstacles: complacency, habitude, ego, and the irresistible tug of the familiar. The economics of the theater promote the idea that an actor is a unit-of-labor purchased at the lowest possible price and then inserted into a larger mechanism which, like him or herself, has limited usefulness and is easily replaceable. But the transient nature of the actor's art is belied by the fact that it has been extant for countless centuries and although generations come and go, varieties of perception contained in timeless artifacts survive in a world without end. That sense of being part of something vast and endlessly renewing is what should give the actor a sense of higher calling which no amount of professional indignity can demean. The actor who feels he is being 'slotted into a role' will act accordingly. The actor who believes that he is being summoned to perform a task which has exercised the keenest sensibilities of both antiquity and modern times, will recognize that only the most strenuous personal effort will qualify him to take his place in the history of the art to which he aspires.

We're all lying in the gutter, said Wilde, but some of us are looking at the stars. The angle of one's head makes all the difference.

EXERCISES

THE MAROWITZ WORK-OUT

"Caesar", Marowitz adaptation of Shake

e's "Julius Caesar", Humboldt Arts Festival

EXERCISES

THE MAROWITZ WORK-OUT

1.   <u>WARM-UP</u>

Place the actors in two parallel lines divided into Group A and Group B. The members of Group A start making movements using only their head and necks; their 'partners' in Group B, as mirror-images, duplicate exactly.

Then Group A initiates movement using only the right hand and right shoulder; Group B duplicates exactly. Then chest, pelvis, both arms, right leg, left leg, both legs, etc are, one by one, brought into the movement. The initiator of the movement should constantly alternate; now Group A then group B and back again. In every case, the movements must be identical both in shape and rhythm.

Group A then initiates hops-in-place, exploring as many kinds of hops as they can invent. Group B follows these movements. Then alternate again with Group B initiating and Group A following, etc.

Group B then initiates Ascents and Descents; ways of moving the entire body up and down. Again, the Initiators alternate between the members of Group A and Group B; first one group initiating and the other following then vice verse.

2. MASKS

Still in parallel lines, Group A flashes out a 'mask' in a fixed expression to their partners in Group B. The mask, like an oriental mask, conveys a very specific mood or emotion. Group A's partners in Group B receiving the mask, answer with a 'mask' of their own which is a reaction to the attitude or emotion projected by the members of Group A. Then Group B initiates the masks and Group A 'reacts.' Eventually, sounds expressing the attitude of each mask are added - until both Initiators and Reactors are conducting, as it were, a dialogue of sounds and masks. At this juncture, the entire body of the performers are incorporated into the changes.

3. THE MAGIC CIRCLE

The group is asked to make a circle as wide as the room. Once this is done, the group is encouraged to observe the persons making up the circle; the difference in height and weight, in attire and deportment, in physiognomy and stance. Once an awareness of the circle has been inculcated, the circle is told that someone, somewhere in the midst of this circle, will initiate a repeated sound-and-movement - something simple and easy to follow - and as soon as that person - whoever he or she may be - initiates that repeated sound-and-movement, the whole circle, as one man, will pick up exactly the same sound-and-movement and, as one unit, draw the circle into the center of the room.

This done, they are told that a contrasting repeated sound-and-movement will bring them all back to the periphery and that as soon as that first person initiates the repeated sound-and-movement, the entire circle, simultaneously duplicating the new sound and movement, and again moving as one man, will return the circle to the periphery. Then another member of the group will initiate yet another contrasting sound-and-movement which will be picked up simultaneously by all, and the circle, continually changing its sounds-and-movements, will again move from the periphery to the center then back to the periphery - and so forth and so on.

4.   THE RHYTHM-EXERCISE

The group remains positioned in a circle as wide as the room. One person in the circle is asked to lay down a fundamental, ground-beat using only vocalized sounds (not music); the kind of constant beat that the percussion-instruments of an orchestra might lay down as a basic rhythmic track. He or she selects this repeated sound and establishes it as the pulse of the exercise which must always be observed.

Then, as they are cued, other members of the group are asked to add to that sound - not by duplicating it, but by creating an interesting augmentation or syncopation of the basic sound. As each member is cued in by the director, the sound develops in elaborateness and richness, always being careful to observe the basic rhythm laid down by the preceding actors. This done, the exercise is repeated with small-scale, tertiary change movements added to the selected sounds.

This done, the exercise is performed again but with the following condition.

Once the group-sounds have been launched and are being rhythmically repeated, the group will, through a kind of osmosis, single out one particular sound-and-movement and then each member of the group will gradually gravitate to that chosen sound-and-movement. Obviously, this is not done by a verbal consensus, but by each member sensing to which sound-and-movement the group is naturally inclining. If one member starts moving in a direction which is contrary to the will of the majority, he must relinquish his selected sound and opt for the choice collectively decided upon. The main point here is that once the selection has been made, each person's individual sound-and-movement must graduate - infinitesmally - to the chosen sound - not leap to it arbitrarily. The transition must pass through a subtle succession of stages, millimeter by millimeter, as it were. Once everyone has joined up to the collectively chosen sound and movement, the person who first initiated it may begin to alter it slightly, the group duplicating those alterations exactly. At a certain point, the Initiator can quietly bring it to a dead halt. The group must follow this progression to a conclusion with all the members of the group working as one person.

The group is then instructed to select a percussive, non-vocalized sound and, as before, this becomes a gradually developing collective rhythm, (One being layered over the other until all have made their contribution.). This done, the exercises is halted and each person given a cue-word which needs to be answered by a responding cue-word: i.e. Light-Dark, Up-Down, In-Out, Round-Flat, Winter-Summer etc. The group is told that when they hear their cue called out (viz. "Light!") they must respond with their cue-word (viz. "Dark!") or, contrariwise, if one hears the cue-word "Dark!," they must respond with *their* cue-word "Light." The calling-out of paired cues ends the exchange.

The percussive, non-vocalized sounds are now repeated by the group. The director circulates around the periphery of the circle and when he taps an actor on the shoulder, they must call out their cue - which summons up the response cue-word from their partner - however, they must not break the rhythm of the exercise they are performing. As the exercise proceeds, the director should circulate faster and faster tapping the actors for their cues and responses in order to create maximum interference in the rhythm of the exercise. Throughout, the rhythm of the exercise must be strictly maintained in spite of the fact that the calling-out of cue-words will constantly subvert it.

The group rhythms can also be composed of flower-names or various diseases. In each case, the chosen word is turned into its sound components and played out as a rhythm not a word - ie. 'gardenia' becomes "*GAR*-deen'yh" - or "Gar-deen-`*YUH*" -- violet' becomes "VY-uhlet' or 'vyuh-`*LET*" etc. In the case of diseases, the group, using illustrative movements, is asked to convey the character of the disease as well as the sound-components of their names - i.e. - 'throm-`*BO*-sis,' 'in-`*SOM*-n'ya' 'in-`*FLU*'en-`*ZUH*', '*WHOOP*-ing-*COUGH*' etc.

In the final version of this exercise, the actor is asked to turn his own name into sound-components (`*PEET*r-Piper - Humpty-`*DUMP*ty - etc) and to express through sound and movement the conception they have of themselves; that is, the kind of person they believe they are. The group, using handclaps, establishes a fixed rhythm for the performer's performance of this exercise. As the group changes its rhythms, the performer must adapt to the changes. This done, the performer will initiate his own changing rhythms and the group will be obliged to adapt themselves accordingly. The director, by clapping his hand on the shoulder of each actor, will designate their entrance into the center of the circle and the start of their name-rhythm.

5. SIMILES

Legato-Staccato:

A circle is formed. Actor A is chosen to initiate a repeated sound-and-movement the overall quality of which is legato; smooth and flow-ing. Actor A goes to the center of the circle and experiments with various sound and movements until he has perfected one that pleases him. He then takes that repeated sound-and-movement and brings it to another member of the company, Actor B. He stands before Actor B still performing his sound-and-movement until he feels Actor B has mastered it perfectly. Then discontinuing the sound-and-movement, he takes Actor B's place. Actor B moves out performing Actor's A's orig-inal sound-and-movement and then gradually, stage by stage, millime-ter by millimeter, transforms its character from a *legato* sound-and-movement to a *staccato* sound-and-movement. Once he has perfected his choices and created the new 'staccato' movement, he brings it to Actor C and when satisfied that Actor C has mastered it, takes his place as Actor C proceeds to transform the *staccato* sound-and-movement into a *legato* sound-and-movement which he then brings to Actor D etc etc and so forth.

Comedy & Tragedy

After an initial eight or ten minutes of the legato-staccato similes, the transformations proceed between Comedy and Tragedy using ex-actly the same format. Here it is important to point out to actors that 'comedy' does not simply mean laughter or 'tragedy,' merely tears, and that the basis of each simile must be a comic or tragic character or a comic or tragic situation - so that the exercise is rooted in specifics and not generalities.

Once the exercise has been launched and maintained for twenty or so minutes, two members should be designated to teach their similes to two other members, each one developing their own (legato-to-staccato staccato-to-legato or comic-to-tragic, tragic-to-comic) and then handing them on to two others. Soon, each member of the company is elaborating one simile or another and there is a gathering sense of chaos as all the similes collide with one another. That is the time to stop the exercise.

6. CHANGING GEARS

Actor A is seated in the center of the room. He is utterly neutral. No one in particular and nowhere in particular. Actor B enters the scene with a line which immediately converts Actor A into a character and places him into a situation, ("I've been having these chest-pains now for over a week."- Actor A is immediately turned into a doctor, Actor B into a patient, the scene, a doctor's consulting-room). After the improvisation has gone for a few moments, Actor C enters the scene with his opening line "How long have you been seeing that woman?," Actor A retires and Actor B adjusts to the new situation in which he is being accused of some marital infidelity and Actor B and C improvise that scene. After a few moments, Actor D enters (again with an entirely unrelated line) triggering an entirely unrelated scene with Actor C and Actor B retires. And so forth and so on. Only two actors should be performing a scene at any given time.

It is best for the director to cue the actors into each scene and to do so just at that point where the scene, after one or two minutes, is reaching some kind of high point. The new actor is always bringing in a new situation and playing with the actor who initiated the previous scene. The scenes and the characters in them are continually changing and hopefully, as radically as possible. The opening line must not be so explicit as to obviate the effect of the scene; for instance, it shouldn't be "How are you Mr. President and what are you doing in this Pentagon office?" It should be just evocative enough to change the scene and suggestive enough to imply a new character and situation without being over-explicit.

7. OLD MAC DONALD HAD A FARM

Most effectively done with a maximum of twelve. The group forms a circle. The First Actor initiates a short, concise movement; the Second Actor repeats it and adds a small addition of his or her own; the Third Actor combines the movements of Actors 1 and 2 and embellishes the movement one step further; the Fourth Actor repeats what is now the assembled movement of Actors 1, 2 & 3 and makes his or her own addition to it. The movement, takes on complexity as it proceeds until it reaches Actor 12 who has the responsibility to perform the whole complex of movements with the final addition of his or her own flourish. Repeat exercise with Actor 12 going to the head of the line as Actor 1 and continue to replace the last actor with the first after each rendition.

8. CHAIN-LINKS

The syllables of a well-known line of Shakespeare (i.e. "To be or not to be that is the question." - "Is this a dagger that I see before me the handle towards my hand?" "O what a rogue and peasant slave am I") are divided between as many actors as there are syllables. The First Actor begins a very distinct rendering of the line using only the first four or five words. He then stops and begins again using only the first syllable - each succeeding actor supplying the remaining syllables of the line and attempting to render it with the same inflection and intention as demonstrated by the First Actor. The First Actor then changes the reading, again using only the first four or five words and the group attempts to fulfill the reading he has begun as faithfully as possible.

The First Actor is then replaced with the last actor and the two actors exchange syllables. The new First Actor now attempts different renderings, this time in a dialect or accent. The actors completing the line are obliged to pick up precisely the dialect or accent adopted by the First Actor. The First Actor is then replaced with the next-to-last actor and so forth and so on, so that each member of the group has an opportunity to initiate the exercise.

Once the company has become adept at assembling the line so that it is no longer a series of broken syllabic fragments but a coherent line as if performed by a single character, the First Actor, again using only the first three or four words of the line, initiates a melody well known to all the members of the group, ("Silent Night" "Happy Birthday," "The National Anthem" "Home Sweet Home" etc.). Once the first few notes of the melody have been sung to the words of the Shakespearean line and the tune grasped, the group attempts to complete the melodic line singing their syllables according to the chosen tune. During the musicalization of the line, it is permissible to extend the syllable by adding extra notes where applicable; that is, to round out the musical phrase. The actual syllable however remains the same. If the melodies chosen are too esoteric, this exercise can easily break down so only well-established and traditional songs should be put to the verse. If it still proves difficult, the group should be encouraged to sing the Shakespearean line *tutti* - in order to hear the way the exercise should sound when executed properly and then returned to the exercise-format.

9. THE PUBLIC LECTURE

The group is seated on the floor. Each member of the group is given a slip of paper on which is inscribed a simple or fanciful lecture-title: e.g. "How To Change A Tire," "My Favorite Deserts," "Why I Believe Abraham Lincoln Was a Woman," "How To Make an Omelet," "Elvis Lives," "My First Sexual Experience," "My Most Memorable Vacation," "Castration: The Answer to Juvenile Crime" etc etc. The group is given three minutes of uninterrupted silence to cogitate the arguments that will make up their public lecture. This done, the actors are assembled in a circle and asked to walk counter-clockwise, very slowly, around the perimeter of the room.

When Actor A is tapped on the shoulder, he must begin delivering his lecture in a loud and clear voice, as it would be projected to an audience that had come especially to hear his oration on that particular subject. When Actor B is tapped on the shoulder and she begins her lecture, Actor A instantaneously cuts out his lecture whether in mid-sentence, mid-word or mid-syllable. When Actor C is tapped and begins his lecture, Actor B instantaneously cuts out her lecture - again, in mid-sentence, mid-word or mid-syllable. But when Actor A or B is tapped again, he or she must resume their lecture precisely at the point where it was interrupted - in mid-sentence, mid-word or mid-syllable. But when he or she hears another lecture begun (because that person has been tapped), he or she must once again cut out wherever the lecture happens to be. As a result of a series of long or short cues given

to actor, the lecture becomes a collage made up of fragments of each actors' lecture.

In the Second Phase, actors are cued one after the other and, instead
of cutting out as before, are told to continue with their lecture. Soon,
each member of the group is delivering his or her lecture simultaneously - all talking at once but concentrated on the gist of their own lectures.

After three or four minutes of simultaneous lectures, the director
reinstates the fragmented lecture-collage, once again tapping actors to
speak and instructing them to desist as soon a they hear another lecture
begun. This collage should have a different pattern from the earlier
one determined by the frequency with which cues (taps on the shoulder) are given.

In the final phase of the exercise, the group is assembled in two or
three rows - like an orchestra. The director explains that they are his
musicians and that they are going to give a concert - however instead of
making music, they are going to perform the words of their lectures,
starting from the very beginning of the talks they have just delivered.
The recitation of the lecture is to be led by the Director exactly as if he
were a conductor and the actors, his orchestra. The tempo is set by the
conductor. Whatever dynamics he wants (legato or staccato, fortissimo
or pianissimo, dolce or bellicoso), it is up to him to convey to his 'orchestra' and for his musicians to convey precisely. After conducting the
simultaneous lectures as a concert-piece for a minute or two (just long
enough for them to get the hang of it), the director retires and selects a
new conductor who is encouraged to draw new tempi and new dynamics from his 'orchestra.' After two or three minutes, that conductor is
replaced by yet another conductor and so forth and so on.

As each actor is appointed conductor, the make-up of the orchestra should change. Under one conductor, there can be a soloist and a quartet separate from the orchestra-proper. The conductor must utilize this new distribution in any way he or she sees fit. In a second permutation, there can be two soloists, a quartet, a can-can line and a ballet-soloist. In each case, they must take their cue from the conductor who must counterpoint their rhythms against the basic rhythm of the group. At all times, the 'music' being performed according to the conductor's tempi, are made up of the words of each member's original lecture, performed according to the rhythms laid down by the respective conductors.

Once every permutation of rhythm and dynamics has been heard and the majority of the group has had their turn as conductors, the exercise is brought to a close.

*   *   *   *   *

INDEX

DIRECTING THE ACTION

by Charles Marowitz

Every actor and director who enters the orbit of this major work will find himself challenged to a deeper understanding of his art and propelled into further realms of exploration. Marowitz mediates on all the sacred precepts of theater practice including auditions, casting, design, rehearsal, actor psychology, dramaturgy and the text.

Directing the Action yields a revised liturgy for all those who would celebrate a theatrical passion on today's stage. But in order to be a disciple in this order, the theater artist must be poised toward piety and heresy at once. Not since Peter Brook's The Empty Space has a major director of such international stature confronted the ancient dilemmas of the stage with such a determined sense of opportunity and discovery.

*"An energizing, uplifting work ... **reading Marowitz on theater is like reading heroic fiction in an age without heroes.**"*
—LOS ANGELES WEEKLY

*"A cogent and incisive collection of ideas, well formulated and clearly set forth; **an important contribution** on directing in postmodern theatre."*
—CHOICE

*"**Consistently thought-provoking** ... sure to be controversial."*
—LIBRARY JOURNAL

paper • ISBN: 1-55783-072-X

APPLAUSE

RECYCLING SHAKESPEARE
by Charles Marowitz

Marowitz' irreverent approach to the bard is destined to outrage Shakespearean scholars across the globe. Marowitz rejects the notion that a "classic" is a sacrosanct entity fixed in time and bounded by its text. A living classic, according to Marowitz, should provoke lively response—even indignation!

In the same way that Shakespeare himself continued to meditate and transform his own ideas and the shape they took, Marowitz gives us license to continue that meditation in productions extrapolated from Shakespeare's work. Shakespeare becomes the greatest of all catalysts who stimulates a constant re-formulation of the fundamental questions of philosophy, history and meaning. Marowitz introduces us to Shakespeare as an active contemporary collaborator who strives with us to yield a vibrant contemporary theatre.

paper • ISBN: 1-55783-094-0

APPLAUSE

ALARUMS & EXCURSIONS

by Charles Marowitz

"Theatre is nothing if it isn't a record of how we thought , and what about. Theatrical journalism, having taken a series of snapshots of the terrain, builds up a picture of a time, a place, an artifact, a set of personalities —all of which enable us to stop the clock long enought to consider where we are going, where we have been, what were we thinikng of then as opposed to now? Examing the finiteness of certain events theoretically helps us understand the nature of the infinite."

From the *Introduction*.

In ALARUMS & EXCURSIONS: OUR THEATRES IN THE 90's, drama critic and stage director Charles Marowitz casts a critical eye upon the highpoints of the last theatrical decade, in preparation for a new millennium. In a series of reviews, think– pieces, and commentaries culled from publications as varied as The London Times and Theatre Week Magazine, Marowitz surveys such watershed productions such as *Oleanna, Angels in America, Phantom of the Opera, The Kentucky Cycle* and *Sunset Boulevard* and the work of such major American playwrights as Mamet, Shepard, Neil Simon, Gurney, Kushner, Baitz, Overmeyer, and McNalley. Marowitz dramatically captures the anger, anxiety, spectacle, and questionable "correctness" that characterized the past decade.

paper • ISBN 1-55783-261-7

APPLAUSE